THE EMOTIONAL COOK

food to match your mood

About Clare McKeon

After studying communications in Dublin and California, where she carried out extensive research into cocktails, Clare headed straight into broadcasting and writing. Ten years on, having presented several primetime radio shows, TV programmes and having written numerous newspaper columns, her professional life is devoted to Food and Drink. As she says herself, 'it's hard work but someone has to do it'. This coincides rather nicely with her serious passions in life – cooking, eating, talking, travelling and raising a racket.

She lives in Dublin with her long-term partner Eamon who will get in a huff, she says, if he doesn't get a mention.

And what does she have to say about her first cookbook? 'I hope it inspires others to become emotional cooks. Don't bottle those feelings – dish 'em out!'

About Eva Byrne

Eva is well-known as a cookery illustrator for magazines and newpapers. Unfortunately, she says, that is where her cooking skills end. On her occasional forays into the kitchen, though, she admits that she too chooses food to match her mood. Eva graduated from the Fashion Institute of Technology, New York, in 1993, where she studied book illustration. She now lives and works in Sligo where she also writes and illustrates children's books.

The Emotional Cook

food to match your mood

CLARE MCKEON

Illustrations by Eva Byrne

THE O'BRIEN PRESS
DUBLIN

First published 1996 by The O'Brien Press Ltd.,
20 Victoria Road, Rathgar, Dublin 6, Ireland

British Library Cataloguing-in-publication Data
McKeon, Clare
The emotional cook: food to match your mood
1.Cookery
I. Title II.Byrne, Eva
641.5

1   2   3   4   5   6   7   8   9   10
96 97 98 99 00 01 02 03 04 05

ISBN: 0-86278-488-3

The publishers wish to acknowledge the following: Recipes for Kitchen Sink Tomato Sandwich
on page 88 and Jailhouse Chilli on page 119 are excerpted from *White Trash Cooking* copyright © 1986
by Ernest Matthew Mickler, with permission from Ten Speed Press, PO Box 7123, Berkeley, CA 94707

The O'Brien Press receives assistance from The Arts Council/An Chomhairle Ealaíon

Cover illustrations: Eva Byrne
Design: Lynn Pierce
Editing: The O'Brien Press Ltd.
Colour separations: Irish Photo Ltd
Printing: Colour Books Ltd.

CONTENTS

INTRODUCTION – **Page 9**

AMOROUS – Oyster Soup 11

Passionfruit Prawns 12

Mango and Cucumber Salad 13

Chocolate-Smothered Strawberries 13

ANGRY – Eggs with Attitude 15

Roaring Red Salsa 16

Sizzling Stir-Fry Beef 16

Curried Vegetables 17

Flaming Bananas 19

BLISSED OUT – Blissful Bloody Marys 21

Chicken Tortillas 21

Mussel Mania 22

Roasted Pepper Salad 23

Potatoes with Anchovy Dressing 23

Heavenly Figs 24

BORED – Spiced Aubergine 25

Tricky Quail 26

Salad with Poppy Seed Dressing 27

CALM – Moroccan Chicken 28

Calming Couscous 29

Mint Tea 30

CONFIDENT – Sophisticates' Soufflé 32

Courgette and Parsley Salad 33

DRAINED – Life-Saving Soup 34

Creamy Dreamy Porridge 35

ENVIOUS – Green-Eyed Soup 36

Pesto Pasta 37

Emerald Salad 37

EXTRAVAGANT – Champagne Risotto 40

Lobster 'n' Lime 42

OTT Pudding 43

FED-UP – The DIY Colonic Irrigation Diet 44

GRATEFUL – The Welcome Drink 46

Surprise Parcels 46

Celebration Lamb 47

Roast Vegetables 48

Portly Prunes 48

GUILTY – Guilt-Free Chocolate Cream 49

HAPPY – Gazpacho 51

Paradisical Paella 52

Nectarina Nirvana 53

HATE – Cunning Corn Chowder 56

Lamb Burgers 57

Wild Mushroom Sauce 57

Sticky Honey Cream 58

HURT – Brown Lentil Soup 60

Chicken Risotto 61

Noodles with Poppy Seed 62

INDULGENT – Creamy Pea Soup 64

Smoked Salmon Pasta 65

Hot Fruit Compote 66

JOVIAL – Mushroom Cappuccino 68

Lettuce Eat Chicken 69

Raspberry Soup 70

KEEN – Asparagus Soup 71

Poached Wild Salmon with Mint Hollandaise Sauce 72

Nutty Ice Cream 73

LONELY – Smoked Mackerel Paté 76

Cucumber Sandwiches **76**

Almond and Orange Pie **77**

Banana Bread **78**

Teacakes **79**

Scones **80**

LOVING – Creamy Vegetable Soup **83**

Lemon Roasted Chicken **84**

Stir-Fry Brussel Sprouts **84**

Mum's Baked Apples **85**

MISCHIEVOUS – Oriental Quail's Eggs **87**

Kitchen Sink Tomato Sandwich **88**

Parsnip Pie Surprise **89**

NOSTALGIC – Oirish Stew **91**

Colcannon **92**

Back to Roots Veg **92**

Bread and Butter Pud **93**

OPTIMISTIC – Outdoors Omelette **95**

Blue Skies Peppers **95**

Picnic Prawns **96**

Hazelnut Dressing **96**

Cheese Al Fresco **96**

PASSIONATE – Frothy Fruit Juice **97**

Orange Pancakes **98**

Passionfruit Yoghurt **99**

Succulent Salmon **99**

QUEASY – Grilled Fish **100**

Grilled Vegetables **100**

Fruit Kebabs 'n' Cream **101**

RAGING – All Steamed-up Seafood **104**

Riot Raisin' Pudding **105**

SAD – Orange Vodka **106**

Cheerful Carrot Soup **107**

Sunny Peppers **108**

Mango Sorbet **108**

Blast from the Past **109**

Sunburst **109**

Sunstroke **109**

STRESSED – Celery Juice **111**

Simple Salad **112**

Tutti-Fruitti **112**

THRILLED – Pear Salad 'n' Dill Dressing **113**

Fiesta Chicken and Salsa Blessed with Te-quila **114**

Pears Poached in Rum **115**

UPSET – Lassi **116**

Smoothie **117**

VULGAR – Jailhouse Chilli **119**

Slow Comfortable Screw **120**

WORRIED – Brown Soda Bread **121**

White Loaf **122**

X-STATIC – Delightful Lime Zing **124**

Pink Flamingoes **124**

Hummus **125**

Creamy Aubergine Mousse **125**

Black Olive Paté **126**

Anchovy Bread **127**

YOUTHFUL – Feed Your Face Mask **128**

Yoghurt and Apple Mask **129**

Avocado and Honey Mask **129**

Eggy Hair Soup **129**

ZESTFUL – Chilled Pepper 'n' Lime Soup **132**

Citrus Sole **132**

Lemon-Scented Rice **133**

Zesty Crêpes **134**

Margharita Springs **135**

INDEX – **137**

DEDICATION

To Eamon with love

ACKNOWLEDGEMENTS

Thanks to:
Eva Byrne for her wonderful, beautiful and evocative illustrations.
Frances Power, my editor, for her insightful comments and vivid imagination.
Marilyn Bright for her expertise on cookery techniques and measurements.
My family and friends for eating experimental dishes and still managing to smile.
Finally and most importantly a huge thanks to my mother, Margaret, who believed in the concept right from the beginning and helped with the research.

INTRODUCTION

That job offer has come through, the baby has arrived. You're on top of the world.
The house-moving is in full throttle, you've been dumped by your partner of twelve years – or two months. You're in a state and the tears are flowing.
So what do you cook up and eat?
No matter what emotional rollercoaster you're on – whether it's Amorous or Zestful – *The Emotional Cook* has a recipe for you. For every crisis life dishes up, there's an appropriate menu. In short, it's food to match your mood.
Will you feel better or worse afterwards?
Hey, there are no guarantees in life, but cooking meals from this cookbook will be fun and different, that's for sure!
The recipes are easy and delicious, if you come across an ingredient you can't get, don't worry, just follow your instincts and substitute something else.
Some of the recipes I picked up on my travels in places like South Africa, Morocco, Long Island, every new trip throws up a new angle on food. Others I've discovered on my own emotional ups and downs.
Don't expect the usual starter, main course, dessert – some emotions demand just chocolate!
Hope you have fun, and remember, when the going gets tough, the tough get cooking!

Here are some important pointers to keep in mind when preparing and cooking food:

- Buy what is fresh, natural and in season
- Be adventurous and inventive
- Keep it simple, don't interfere with the food too much
- Trust your instinct, not the recipe
- Use natural sea salt and use it sparingly
- Sugar is a no-no, try honey or maple syrup instead
- Always freshly mill your black pepper
- Use extra virgin oil, cold pressed
- Eat healthy wholefood, diets are a bad joke
- Death to artificial fizzy drinks!
- Resist serving plonky wine to your guests
- Garlic is where it's at
- Quality not quantity
- Organic and free range foods are the best option
- The taste of food is a personal thing, season the way *you* want
- Five portions of fruit and vegetables per person per day is healthy

Clare McKeon
August 1996

Cooking is like love. It should be entered into with abandon
or not at all.
Harriet van Horne

For that first serious at-home date. But, be realistic, I'm not talking fatal attraction here. If it's necessary to kidnap or tie and blindfold your guest then I think you may be wasting your time. Your intended must be interested but as yet no moves have been made. This menu is meant to push interested towards amorously inclined.

First, forget all that rot talked about aphrodisiacs – rhino horn, tiger penis, bird's nest soup. No thank you. Try oysters – the ultimate seduction food – and a touch of extravagance with champagne, seafood and the sensuous texture of strawberries and chocolate. Good honest lurve food.

Next, keep the following in mind:

- You've got to eat lightly – lust does not prosper on a full stomach
- Lust does not do too well on a body low in energy either
- Watch your alcohol intake – drink may fuel your ambitions, but brewer's droop is no fable, or so I'm told.

OYSTER SOUP

SERVES 2

12 OYSTERS

1 TABLESPOON OLIVE OIL

2 SHALLOTS, CHOPPED

110 ML/4 FL OZ/$\frac{1}{2}$ CUP CHAMPAGNE

225 ML/8 FL OZ/1 CUP VEGETABLE STOCK

1 POTATO, COOKED AND MASHED

FRESHLY GROUND BLACK PEPPER

1 TEASPOON FRESH PARSLEY, CHOPPED

OYSTER KNIFE OR SMALL STRONG KNIFE

- **WRAP** HANDS WITH DISHCLOTH OR **WEAR** RUBBER GLOVES FOR PROTECTION.
- **PLACE** OYSTER SHELL ON WORK SURFACE — IF SLIGHTLY OPEN, **DISCARD**.
- **INSERT** OYSTER KNIFE INTO HINGE AT BACK OF SHELL.
- **PUSH** HARD, THEN **TWIST** (**DO NOT LOSE** JUICES).
- **PLACE** OYSTER AND JUICE IN BOWL.
- **REPEAT** FOR EACH OYSTER.
- **HEAT** OLIVE OIL IN PAN.
- **SAUTÉ** SHALLOTS UNTIL PALE AND SOFT.
- **POUR** IN CHAMPAGNE AND VEGETABLE STOCK.
- **SIMMER** TO REDUCE TO HALF.
- **ADD** POTATO.
- **BRING** TO BOIL.
- **ADD** OYSTERS AND JUICES.
- **STIR** FOR ABOUT 10 MINUTES (**DO NOT BOIL**).
- **ADD** PEPPER TO TASTE.
- **SERVE** WITH SPRINKLING OF PARSLEY.

PASSIONFRUIT PRAWNS

SERVES 2

14 LARGE UNCOOKED PRAWNS

3 TABLESPOONS OLIVE OIL

1 TABLESPOON CIDER VINEGAR

1 RIPE PASSIONFRUIT

- **STEAM** PRAWNS FOR 3 MINUTES UNTIL PINK.
- **COOL, REMOVE** SHELLS AND **DISCARD**.
- **MIX** OIL AND VINEGAR IN BOWL.
- **HALVE** PASSIONFRUIT AND **SCOOP OUT** INSIDES.
- **MASH, ADD** TO OIL AND VINEGAR AND **MIX** WELL.
- **ADD** PRAWNS.
- **MARINATE** FOR 10 MINUTES.
- **SERVE** PRAWNS ON BED OF MANGO AND CUCUMBER SALAD.

Mango and Cucumber Salad

SERVES 2

1 RIPE MANGO, PEELED AND DICED

1 CUCUMBER, VERY FINELY SLICED

1 HEAD OF LETTUCE, SHREDDED

- **MIX** MANGO AND CUCUMBER IN BOWL.
- **ADD** LETTUCE.
- **SERVE.**

Chocolate-Smothered Strawberries

SERVES 2

15-20 STRAWBERRIES

85 G/3 OZ DARK CHOCOLATE

170 ML/6 FL OZ/$\frac{3}{4}$ CUP DOUBLE CREAM

- **WASH** AND **HULL** STRAWBERRIES.
- **PAT** DRY WITH KITCHEN PAPER.
- **MELT** CHOCOLATE IN BOWL OVER BARELY SIMMERING WATER.
- **HEAT** CREAM IN ANOTHER SAUCEPAN.
- **ADD** CHOCOLATE TO CREAM, STIRRING.
- **POUR** SAUCE OVER STRAWBERRIES AND **DEVOUR.**

To drink? Champagne, naturally!

ANGRY

When he is late for dinner and I know he must be either having an affair or lying dead in the street, I always hope he's dead.
Judith Viorst

Anger reminds me of a volcano. It can simmer and bubble for a while like a pressure cooker before it gets up to full steam. Or it can explode suddenly and without warning. Some of us can cover up our anger and maintain a calm exterior, while inside a white-hot core of emotion boils, barely suppressed, just waiting for that little nudge to spill over. Others of us are more 'Latin', flying off the handle at the smallest of things and cooling down within seconds so that we can't even remember what it was that made us so angry.

My advice is: don't bottle it. You could deal with it yourself in a number of ways – chop logs, lift weights in a gym, scream. Interesting therapy, and you could lose a foot, bust a gut or strain your voice. I don't think so. There's another more satisfying route to take that involves channelling your anger into activity and creativity. That is to get into the kitchen and get cooking. Anger gives a bit of an edge to your cooking and you'll find that the dishes created out of this mood are tasty, memorable and have a certain *oomph!* Food with attitude.

Channelling is the key word here. It means you must force restraint on yourself, otherwise you'll never peel that garlic and you'll certainly never crack the eggs properly. Channel the anger and control it, converting it into activity that will dissipate the bulk of those negative feelings. By the time the food is cooked you'll have calmed down and be ready to eat.

If not, serve it to someone else, as it's not good to eat on an angry stomach.

EGGS WITH ATTITUDE

SERVES 2

2 TABLESPOONS OLIVE OIL

1 LARGE ONION, CHOPPED

1 CLOVE GARLIC, CRUSHED

3 MEDIUM POTATOES, STEAMED
WITH SKINS ON AND COARSELY CHOPPED

2 COURGETTES, CHOPPED

½ RED AND ½ GREEN PEPPER, CHOPPED

3 FREE RANGE EGGS, BEATEN

55 ML/2 FL OZ/¼ CUP SOURED CREAM

1 TEASPOON BLACK PEPPER

2 TEASPOONS NUTMEG

PINCH OF SEA SALT

- **PRE-HEAT** OVEN TO 180°C/350°F/GAS MARK 4.
- **GREASE** 15 CM/6 INCH SPRINGFORM TIN.
- **HEAT** PAN WITH DROP OF OLIVE OIL.
- **ADD** ONION AND GARLIC.
- **SAUTÉ** FOR 2 MINUTES.
- **ADD** POTATOES, COURGETTES AND PEPPERS.
- **COOK** UNTIL SOFT.
- **COMBINE** IN BOWL WITH REST OF INGREDIENTS.
- **SEASON.**
- **PUT** MIXTURE IN PAN IN OVEN.
- **BAKE** FOR 20 MINUTES OR UNTIL FIRM.
- **SERVE** WITH ROARING RED SALSA.

ROARING RED SALSA

SERVES 2

$\frac{1}{2}$ RED HOT CHILLI PEPPER

1 YELLOW BELL PEPPER

3 RIPE TOMATOES

1 SMALL RED ONION

1 CLOVE GARLIC, PEELED

JUICE OF 1 LIME

- **DE-SEED** AND **CHOP** CHILLI PEPPER (**DO NOT TOUCH** YOUR FACE AS RESIDUE FROM SEEDS AND SKIN CAN CAUSE SEVERE IRRITATION).
- **DE-SEED** YELLOW PEPPER AND **CHOP** ROUGHLY.
- **WHIZZ** ALL INGREDIENTS IN PROCESSOR.
- **COVER** AND **REFRIGERATE** UNTIL YOU SERVE.

SIZZLING STIR-FRY BEEF

SERVES 2

175 G/6 OZ SIRLOIN STEAK

2 TABLESPOONS SOY SAUCE

1-2 CLOVES GARLIC, CRUSHED

2 TABLESPOONS SESAME OIL

2 TABLESPOONS PEANUT OIL (GROUNDNUT OIL)

1 LARGE ONION, THINLY SLICED

1 TABLESPOON GINGER ROOT, PEELED AND GRATED

55 G/2 OZ MANGE-TOUT PEAS

- **TENDERISE** STEAK BY THUMPING WITH WOODEN SPOON.
- **SLICE** ACROSS GRAIN AND **CUT** INTO BITE-SIZED STRIPS.
- **MARINATE** IN SOY SAUCE FOR 20 MINUTES WITH CRUSHED GARLIC AND SESAME OIL.
- **HEAT** HALF OF PEANUT OIL IN WOK ON HIGHEST HEAT.
- **ADD** ONION AND GINGER.
- **REMOVE** TO ANOTHER DISH AFTER 2 MINUTES.

- **PUT** REMAINDER OF PEANUT OIL IN WOK.

- **STIR-FRY** BEEF WITH MARINADE.

- WHEN BEEF IS COOKED, **ADD** IN ONIONS AND GINGER.

- **ADD** MANGE-TOUT FOR LAST MINUTE OF COOKING (**DO NOT COOK** FOR MORE THAN 1 MINUTE AS THEY WILL BECOME SOGGY AND LOSE THEIR GREENNESS).

- **SERVE** DIRECTLY FROM WOK.

CURRIED VEGETABLES

SERVES 2

1 TABLESPOON SUNFLOWER OIL

1 MEDIUM ONION, SLICED

5 BRUSSEL SPROUTS, SLICED

2 SMALL CARROTS, SLICED

4 MEDIUM CAULIFLOWER FLORETS, SLICED

$\frac{1}{4}$ TEASPOON TURMERIC

2 TABLESPOONS CURRY POWDER

1 CAN TOMATOES

1 SMALL GREEN CHILLI PEPPER, DE-SEEDED AND CHOPPED

1 GARLIC CLOVE, CRUSHED

140 ML/5 FL OZ/$\frac{2}{3}$ CUP BOILING WATER

- **HEAT** OIL IN LARGE PAN.

- **SAUTÉ** ONIONS.

- WHEN BROWN, **ADD** BRUSSEL SPROUTS, CARROTS AND CAULIFLOWER.

- **ADD** TURMERIC AND CURRY POWDER.

- **COAT** VEGETABLES WITH SPICES.

- **STIR** IN TOMATOES, GREEN CHILLI PEPPER AND GARLIC.

- **ADD** BOILING WATER.

- **SIMMER** FOR ABOUT 20 MINUTES OR UNTIL VEGETABLES ARE TENDER.

- **SERVE** AS SIDE DISH WITH SIZZLING STIR-FRY BEEF.

FLAMING BANANAS

SERVES 2

2 BANANAS

JUICE OF $\frac{1}{2}$ ORANGE

55 ML/2 FL OZ/$\frac{1}{4}$ CUP MAPLE SYRUP

55 ML/2 FL OZ/$\frac{1}{4}$ CUP BRANDY

DOLLOP OF CRÈME FRAÎCHE

- **CUT** BANANAS LENGTHWAYS.
- **PLACE** IN FRYING-PAN OR WOK WITH ORANGE JUICE AND MAPLE SYRUP.
- **SIMMER** FOR 5 MINUTES.
- **POUR** HALF OF BRANDY OVER BANANAS.
- **POUR** REMAINING BRANDY INTO SMALL SAUCEPAN AND **WARM** GENTLY.
- **REMOVE** FROM HEAT.
- **POUR** HEATED BRANDY OVER BANANAS.
- **SET** ALIGHT (**DO NOT SMELL** OR **TASTE** UNTIL FLAMES HAVE DIED DOWN, AND **WATCH OUT** FOR SINGEING EYELASHES).
- **PLACE** BANANAS AND SAUCE ON WARM PLATE.
- **SERVE** WITH A SPOONFUL OF CRÈME FRAÎCHE.

To drink: a full-bodied Australian Chardonnay or a chilled beer.

BLISSED OUT

If ignorance is bliss why aren't more people happy?
Leonard Rossiter

Can life be this good? Oh yes it can, and if things are going well why not celebrate with friends and do brunch? Need I emphasis that all the guests should be *good* friends – it's just not worth inviting potential troublemakers: drunks, compulsive joketellers or loud-mouth bores.

Why brunch?

Well, if you're in a great mood then the spontaneity of an informal group is just the thing. You automatically have the mingle factor. Guests will swap and chop and change among themselves according to the conversation, the mood or the food that has just been served. To encourage mingling, guests are served buffet style, and to discourage washing-up, they help themselves, eating with their fingers or a fork.

Surroundings are crucial. Plenty of light is a must, so make sure you choose a room that catches the light at this time of day. Don't forget fresh flowers. Have candles on standby, as a late afternoon chill or gloom may settle, and candles are a sure antidote to any reduction in the atmosphere. Here's my tip for making candles last longer: chill in the freezer for 10 minutes before you light them. They'll burn more slowly.

And you might be surprised that I'm pointing this out but make sure the room or rooms are warm. I've lost count of the houses I've visited in which my feet have been blocks of ice. I have even been known to over-indulge in alcohol in a desperate attempt to compensate for the frigid atmosphere. People who can't heat their rooms properly should *not* be allowed to host parties!

The best way to get a brunch off to a roaring start is to serve up a great cocktail. I go for Bloody Marys, relaxed and laid-back with a kick. But unless you make a good one don't even bother to begin. This particular Bloody Mary is well worth the effort, so here goes:

BLISSFUL BLOODY MARYS

SERVES 12

3 X 400 G CANS TOMATOES, WITH JUICE

1 RED ONION, THINLY SLICED

½ RED PEPPER, THINLY SLICED

4 CLOVES GARLIC, PEELED

10 SHAKES TABASCO SAUCE

4 SHAKES WORCESTER SAUCE

25 G/1 OZ FRESH HORSERADISH, GRATED

FRESHLY GROUND BLACK PEPPER

JUICE OF 1 LIME

570 ML/1 PINT/2½ CUPS VODKA

12 STICKS CELERY

- **PUT** EVERYTHING EXCEPT VODKA INTO PROCESSOR.
- **WHIZZ** UNTIL SMOOTH.
- **POUR** IN VODKA AND **GIVE** ANOTHER WHIZZ TO BLEND EVENLY.
- **SERVE** OVER ICE WITH STICK OF CELERY.

After a few of these your guests should be experiencing a fairly strong feeling of bliss.

Now, on to the food and a brunch menu that allows guests to help themselves from a selection of dishes.

CHICKEN TORTILLAS

SERVES 12

4 RED ONIONS, SLICED FINELY

1 LARGE RED PEPPER, SLICED IN THIN STRIPS

2 CLOVES GARLIC, CRUSHED

1.8 KG/4 LBS COOKED CHICKEN, SKINLESS AND SLICED

JUICE OF 6 LIMES

24 FLOUR TORTILLAS, READY-MADE

450 ML/16 FL OZ/2 CUPS SALSA (SEE 'ANGER' FOR RECIPE)

450 ML/16 FL OZ/2 CUPS SOURED CREAM

- **Heat** oil in large cast-iron frying-pan.
- **Add** onions and red pepper.
- **Fry** until soft.
- **Take** out of frying-pan and **put** to one side.
- **Reheat** frying-pan and **add** garlic.
- **Add** chicken strips and lime juice.
- **Simmer** and **reduce** juice until thickened.
- **Heat** tortillas by steaming over water in bamboo steamer.
- **Organise** salsa and soured cream in separate dishes.
- **Place** chicken in bowl alongside flour tortillas.
- **Place** onions and peppers in another dish.
- **Get** guests to form a tortilla assembly line.
- **Fill** each tortilla with a selection of chicken, soured cream and salsa.
- **Roll** tortilla up and **eat**.

Mussel Mania

Serves 12

60 mussels (5 per person)

2 tablespoons olive oil

2 medium onions, finely chopped

4 cloves garlic, crushed

450 ml/16 fl oz/2 cups white wine

juice of 2 lemons

1 bunch fresh coriander, chopped

- **Prepare** mussels by washing and scrubbing shells in cold water.
- **Scrape** away barnacles.
- **Discard** any mussels that are already open.
- **Heat** oil in large pot.
- **Add** onion and garlic.
- **Sauté** for 3 minutes.
- **Pour** in white wine.

- ADD mussels and **SIMMER** until mussels open (3-5 minutes).
- ADD lemon juice and coriander.
- AFTER cooking **THROW AWAY** any mussels still closed.
- SERVE steaming hot on large plate with plenty of crusty bread.

ROASTED PEPPER SALAD

SERVES 12

3 RED PEPPERS

3 GREEN PEPPERS

3 YELLOW PEPPERS

20 BLACK OLIVES

1 TABLESPOON CAPERS

4 TABLESPOONS OLIVE OIL

2 TABLESPOONS BALSAMIC VINEGAR

- PRE-HEAT oven to 180°C/350°F/Gas Mark 4.
- BAKE whole peppers for 30 minutes or until skin is blackened and blistered.
- REMOVE and **PLACE** in polythene bag and **SEAL**.
- WAIT 30 minutes and then **SKIN**.
- PEEL and **DE-SEED** peppers.
- CUT into strips and **PLACE** in salad bowl.
- ADD olives and capers.
- MIX well.
- SPRINKLE with oil and vinegar.

POTATOES WITH ANCHOVY DRESSING

SERVES 12

1 KG/2¼ LB SMALL POTATOES

6 ANCHOVIES, FINELY CHOPPED

2 TABLESPOONS DIJON MUSTARD

BUNCH FRESH PARSLEY, CHOPPED

4 TABLESPOONS BALSAMIC VINEGAR

4 TABLESPOONS OLIVE OIL

JUICE OF 1 LEMON

12 SMALL GHERKINS, CHOPPED

- **STEAM** AND **QUARTER** POTATOES INTO SERVING DISH.
- **MIX** ANCHOVIES, MUSTARD AND PARSLEY IN BOWL.
- **STIR** IN VINEGAR, OIL AND LEMON JUICE.
- **ADD** GHERKINS TO POTATOES AND **POUR** DRESSING OVER.
- **SERVE.**

HEAVENLY FIGS

SERVES 12

24 RIPE FIGS

4 TABLESPOONS HONEY

225 ML/8 FL OZ/1 CUP ORANGE JUICE

140 ML/5 FL OZ/$\frac{2}{3}$ CUP BRANDY

12 TABLESPOONS MASCARPONE CHEESE

$\frac{1}{2}$ TEASPOON POPPY SEEDS

- **PRE-HEAT** OVEN TO 180°C/350°F/GAS MARK 4.
- **CUT** FIGS IN HALF.
- **PLACE** IN GREASED OVENPROOF DISH.
- **MIX** HONEY AND ORANGE JUICE TOGETHER, THEN **MIX** WITH BRANDY.
- **POUR** OVER FIGS.
- **BAKE** FOR 20 MINUTES.
- **MIX** CHEESE WITH POPPY SEEDS IN BOWL.
- **ARRANGE** FIGS IN SERVING DISH.
- **PLACE** CHEESE AROUND FIGS.
- **LET** GUESTS **HELP** THEMSELVES.

BORED

Wet Sunday afternoons are the killer for me. The television offers only sport or old black and white movies as an antidote. Even the Sunday papers seem jaded and tired. It's too wet and miserable to go out anywhere, and too boring to stay in.

Add hunger to your boredom and you're in a vulnerable state, you are in danger of ending up in front of the TV spooning cold beans into yourself. Couch potato time.

What's needed is some action. Counteract that boredom with a spot of fiddly food.

You can't cook just any old thing – if the remedy to boredom was that simple you could just shove a turkey in the oven. But it doesn't work that way. So jazz yourself up and throw a casual dinner party for six. Put in an effort which will pay dividends, in the way of positive feedback and glowing tributes from your guests. Superwoman Shirley Conran says life is too short to stuff a mushroom, but when boredom sets in there's plenty of time to stuff a quail.

SPICED AUBERGINE

SERVES 6

6 TABLESPOONS OLIVE OIL

$\frac{1}{2}$ TEASPOON CUMIN SEEDS

$\frac{1}{2}$ TEASPOON CORIANDER SEEDS

4 TOMATOES, SKINNED AND CHOPPED

2 CLOVES GARLIC, CRUSHED

1 TABLESPOON ROOT GINGER, PEELED AND GRATED

$\frac{1}{2}$ TEASPOON TURMERIC

2 MEDIUM AUBERGINES, DICED

LETTUCE TO GARNISH

BROWN SODA BREAD

- HEAT OIL.
- ADD CUMIN AND CORIANDER.
- HEAT TO SIZZLE POINT.
- ADD TOMATOES, GARLIC, GINGER AND TURMERIC.
- COOK TO A THICK PASTE.
- ADD AUBERGINE.
- COVER AND COOK ON LOW HEAT UNTIL SOFT (ABOUT 30 MINUTES).
- SERVE ON BED OF LETTUCE WITH SLICED SODA BREAD (SEE 'WORRIED' FOR RECIPE).

TRICKY QUAIL

SERVES 6

350 G/12 OZ DRIED WILD MUSHROOMS (MORELS ARE GOOD)

12 QUAIL, 2 PER PERSON

OLIVE OIL

3 TABLESPOONS CRÈME FRAÎCHE

FRESHLY GROUND BLACK PEPPER

- **PRE-HEAT** OVEN TO 180°C/350°F/GAS MARK 4.
- **PLACE** MUSHROOMS IN BOWL.
- **POUR** ENOUGH BOILING WATER OVER MUSHROOMS TO COVER.
- **SOAK** FOR 15 MINUTES.
- **DRAIN** WATER AND **RETAIN** FOR SAUCE.
- **STUFF** QUAILS WITH MUSHROOMS.
- **BRUSH** WITH OLIVE OIL AND **PLACE** IN ROASTING TIN.
- **ROAST** FOR 25 MINUTES.
- **REMOVE** QUAIL TO SERVING DISH AND **KEEP** WARM.
- **POUR** MUSHROOM WATER IN PAN AND **BOIL** TO REDUCE LIQUID.
- WHEN LIQUID HAS REDUCED BY HALF, **ADD** CRÈME FRAÎCHE.
- **CONTINUE TO REDUCE** OVER HIGH HEAT.
- **SERVE** ON POOL OF SAUCE WITH GREEN SALAD.
- **SPRINKLE** WITH BLACK PEPPER.

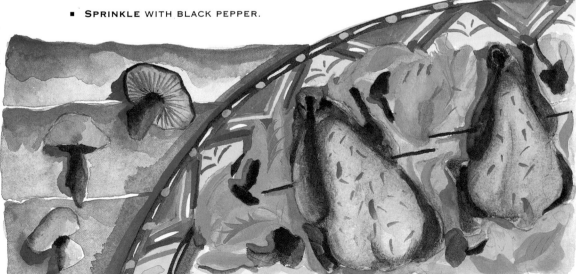

SALAD WITH POPPY SEED DRESSING

SERVES 6

MIXED SALAD LEAVES

5 TABLESPOONS OLIVE OIL

2 TABLESPOONS BALSAMIC VINEGAR

1 HEAPED TABLESPOON POPPY SEEDS

- **WASH** AND **PREPARE** SALAD LEAVES.
- **WHISK** OTHER INGREDIENTS TOGETHER.
- **POUR** DRESSING OVER LEAVES.
- **SERVE** WITH QUAIL.

To drink: a Pinot Noir from Italy or South Africa

For dessert serve a selection of Irish farmhouse cheeses – Cashel Blue, Gubeen, Milleens or perhaps some Cooleeney. Serve with a glass of dessert wine, anything except a syrupy French Muscat. A nice Sauternes should do the trick, or my favourite, a bottle of Brown Brothers Orange Blossom Muscat from Australia. The most jaded of palates will be pleasantly surprised.

There is no joy but calm.
'The Lotus Eaters', Alfred, Lord Tennyson

The question is whether or not you should do anything at all. Why disturb a tranquil pond?

We all have to eat though, and what better way to approach certain recipes than a calm self-assuredness. My choice would be a meal which has just one course and cooks in one pot. Now that sounds calm-inducing, doesn't it? No fuss.

A few years ago, while visiting Agadir, I was lucky enough to be invited into the home of a large extended Moroccan family. A Moroccan household, I thought, would be bustling, noisy, full of life. Wrong. The first thing that struck me (apart from the sheer number of people, from toddlers to the fierce old matriarchal grandmother) was the all-pervading sense of calm that permeated the house. The inhabitants were in the habit of leaving their daily troubles at the doorstep. This was the custom, and the atmosphere that was encouraged (by the women of the house, I might add) was one of serenity.

The entire evening revolved around a large communal meal. Family members busied themselves with their domestic chores, and eventually everyone met at the large low table. The food had been cooking sedately for a number of hours and even the sense of frantic deadlines that hits many cooks when preparing for large numbers was absent from the women who graciously served up a mouth-watering dish of chicken with olives and lemon. Here's my interpretation of that dish:

MOROCCAN CHICKEN

SERVES 6

1 TABLESPOON PEANUT OIL (GROUNDNUT OIL)

1.35KG/3 LB CHICKEN, CUT INTO 8 PIECES

2 LARGE ONIONS, GRATED

2 GARLIC CLOVES, CRUSHED

1/2 TEASPOON SAFFRON

1 TEASPOON CINNAMON

140 ML/5 FL OZ/2/3 CUP WATER

2 LEMONS, QUARTERED

30 KALAMATA OLIVES

- **PRE-HEAT** OVEN TO 160°C/325°F/GAS MARK 3.
- **HEAT** OIL IN HEAVY-BOTTOMED CASSEROLE DISH.
- **ADD** CHICKEN.
- **BROWN** LIGHTLY ON ALL SIDES.
- **ADD** ONION, GARLIC AND SPICES.
- **COOK** FOR 5 MINUTES.
- **ADD** WATER.
- **ADD** QUARTERED LEMONS AND OLIVES AND **COVER**.
- **PLACE** IN OVEN.
- **COOK** FOR 2 HOURS.
- **SERVE** WITH BREAD TO SOAK UP JUICES.
- **EAT** WITH FINGERS OF YOUR RIGHT HAND ONLY, IF YOU WANT TO OBSERVE TRUE MOROCCAN CUSTOM.

What potatoes are to Ireland, pasta is to Italy, and rice is to China – that's what couscous is to Morocco.

CALMING COUSCOUS

SERVES 6
350 G/12 OZ/2 CUPS COUSCOUS
725 ML/1 ¼ PINTS/3 CUPS VEGETABLE STOCK
8 CARROTS, SCRUBBED

- **PUT** COUSCOUS IN LARGE BOWL.
- **POUR** IN HOT VEGETABLE STOCK.
- **STIR** THOROUGHLY.
- **LEAVE** FOR 30 MINUTES.
- **DRAIN**.
- **PLACE** COUSCOUS IN STEAMER LINED WITH MUSLIN.
- **PUT** WHOLE CARROTS ON TOP.
- **STEAM** FOR 20 MINUTES.
- **ARRANGE** COUSCOUS IN A MOUND, AND **STICK** CARROTS IN AT ANGLES.
- **SERVE** STEAMING HOT.

There is only one drink to take with this meal – mint tea. The markets in Morocco are full of bundles of fresh mint. It looks and smells exquisite and makes a cooling and refreshing drink. It also aids digestion. The only problem is that when Moroccans make mint tea they add a truckload of sugar. We're talking sickly sweet here. Why not try mint tea with a kick and add a measure of whisky or tequila instead of sugar?

MINT TEA

FOR EACH CUP TAKE A HANDFUL OF FRESH MINT

- **PLACE** MINT IN HEAT-RESISTANT GLASS.
- **POUR** BOILING WATER ON MINT.
- **ADD** A DASH OF ALCOHOL.
- **WRAP** GLASS IN NAPKIN.
- **SERVE.**

C O N F I D E N T

I am an enormously talented man, after all
it's no use pretending that I am not, and I was bound to succeed.
Noël Coward

You might feel a little nervous about concocting a dish you have never tried before. Why do you think cookery shows on TV are so popular? We watch these to see how *proper* cooking is done and then imagine that some day we might be up to it. Never in our wildest dreams do we imagine that we could just as easily be sizzling food in that wok, or flambée-ing with such panache.

Confidence is the key, and the key to confidence is to push the boat out in terms of what you believe you can do! Don't be afraid to make mistakes. Family members are good to practise on, even if it's a disaster they'll still be grateful for the effort you have made.

Let's face it, the soufflé has always been surrounded by mystique. According to cooking lore it's one of the trickiest dishes to get right and novice cooks are warned to stay well away. But with a little confidence ...

Here are three key points to remember when making a soufflé:

1. The oven must always be pre-heated

2. The bowl you use to whisk the egg whites in must be dry and very clean

3. You must serve your creation the instant it comes out of the oven

What's great about this recipe is that the soufflé rises in its own cunning container – the red pepper.

SOPHISTICATES' SOUFFLÉ

SERVES 4

4 RED PEPPERS, DE-SEEDED WITH TOPS CUT OFF

2 TABLESPOONS BUTTER

3 TABLESPOONS PLAIN FLOUR

225 ML/8 FL OZ/1 CUP MILK

3 FREE RANGE EGGS, SEPARATED

1 TABLESPOON OLIVE OIL

1 SMALL ONION, VERY FINELY CHOPPED

3 MEDIUM TOMATOES, SKINNED AND CHOPPED

LARGE PINCH OF SEA SALT

FRESHLY GROUND BLACK PEPPER

4 TABLESPOONS PARMESAN, GRATED

LETTUCE LEAVES TO GARNISH

- PRE-HEAT OVEN TO 200°C/400°F/GAS MARK 6.
- STAND PEPPERS – PROP UPRIGHT WITH CRUMPLED FOIL – ON BAKING SHEET.
- HEAT BUTTER IN PAN.
- ADD FLOUR.
- STIR AND COOK FOR 1 MINUTE.
- REMOVE FROM HEAT.
- BEAT IN MILK LITTLE BY LITTLE.
- SIMMER AND STIR CONTINUOUSLY UNTIL SAUCE IS THICK.
- REMOVE FROM HEAT AND ALLOW TO COOL.
- BEAT EGG YOLKS.
- ADD TO COOLED SAUCE.
- SAUTÉ ONION AND TOMATO IN OLIVE OIL FOR 5 MINUTES.
- ADD TO COOLED SAUCE, PLUS SEA SALT AND BLACK PEPPER.
- WHISK EGG WHITES IN BOWL UNTIL STIFF.
- FOLD 2 TABLESPOONS OF EGG WHITE INTO TOMATO AND ONION SAUCE WITH A METAL SPOON.
- FOLD IN REMAINING EGG WHITES GENTLY.
- SPOON MIXTURE INTO PREPARED PEPPERS.

- **SPRINKLE** WITH PARMESAN CHEESE.

- **BAKE** IN OVEN FOR 30 MINUTES WITH LIDS.

- **SERVE** IMMEDIATELY, TOPPED WITH LIDS, SURROUNDED BY A SELECTION OF LETTUCE LEAVES.

Now to take a different tack. It takes real confidence to serve up a very simple dish. Pile strips of courgette onto a bed of parsley, topped with shavings of parmesan cheese

COURGETTE AND PARSLEY SALAD

SERVES 4

8 LARGE CLOVES GARLIC

4 TABLESPOONS OLIVE OIL

1 TABLESPOON LEMON JUICE

FRESHLY GROUND BLACK PEPPER

2 MEDIUM COURGETTES

2 STICKS CELERY, FINELY SLICED

85 G/3 OZ/$\frac{1}{2}$ CUP FRESH PARSLEY, CHOPPED

PARMESAN SHAVINGS TO GARNISH

PARSLEY TO GARNISH

- **PUT** WHOLE GARLIC CLOVES IN SAUCEPAN.

- **COVER** WITH WATER.

- **SIMMER** FOR 20 MINUTES.

- **DRAIN** AND **COOL**.

- **REMOVE** SKINS.

- **PRESS** GARLIC THROUGH SIEVE TO MAKE PURÉE.

- **WHISK** PURÉE WITH OIL, LEMON JUICE AND PEPPER.

- **TRIM** COURGETTE AND **GRATE** COARSELY.

- **MIX** WITH CELERY AND GARLIC DRESSING.

- **SERVE** TOPPED WITH PARMESAN ON BED OF PARSLEY.

To drink: a Sauvignon Blanc from New Zealand

DRAINED

Life is just one damned thing after another.
Elbert Hubbard

We've all felt this way. There seems to be a hassle around every corner. The very last thing you needed was a friend laying a trip on you about unimportant trivia. But it's happened. You can't take any more – you're emotionally and physically drained. You do the best you can, juggling and managing an increasing emotional overload. You arrive home, fire your bag in the corner, throw your coat over the back of the chair and flop down into an armchair, kicking your shoes off. You're done for. My first word of advice in such a situation is that your only duty at this stage is to yourself. Do not even consider preparing and cooking food for anyone else, especially a partner or other family members. This would be mental suicide and would drain the last of your energy. What is needed here is quickie food for one person. And try to avoid alcohol, it will just make you feel worse.

This is an extremely restorative soup. Miso comes in a wide variety of flavours and strengths. Some misos are made from barley, others from rice or chickpeas. The best soup miso is genmai which is made from fermented soya and brown rice.

LIFE-SAVING SOUP

SERVES 1

3 TEASPOONS EDIBLE SEAWEED, EG DILLISK

570 ML/1 PINT/2 ½ CUPS WATER

1 TEASPOON MISO

1 SPRING ONION, CHOPPED

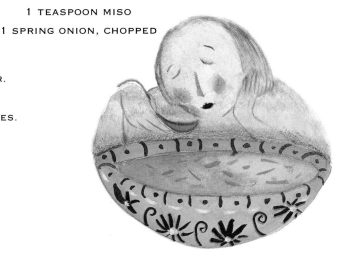

- **CHOP** SEAWEED.
- **ADD** TO BOILING WATER.
- **BRING** BACK TO BOIL.
- **SIMMER** FOR 10 MINUTES.
- **REMOVE** FROM HEAT.
- **ADD** MISO.
- **DO NOT BOIL.**
- **ADD** SPRING ONIONS.
- **DRINK.**

Before you face into the storm again, fortify yourself with some fighting food.

CREAMY DREAMY PORRIDGE

SERVES 1

4 TABLESPOONS OATFLAKES

170 ML/6 FL OZ/¾ CUP WATER

1 TABLESPOON HONEY

CREAM OR MILK

- **PUT** WATER AND OATFLAKES IN SAUCEPAN.
- **BOIL** AND **STIR** CONSTANTLY FOR ABOUT 4 MINUTES.
- **STIR** IN HONEY.
- **TAKE OFF** HEAT.
- **POUR** INTO BOWL.
- **EAT** WITH LASHINGS OF CREAM OR, FOR THE FAINT-HEARTED, SOME MILK.

E N V I O U S

If envy were a fever, all the world would be ill.
Danish proverb

This green-eyed pixie is a real killer. It can invade your system and camp out like an unwelcome squatter in your gut. The only way to get rid of this demon is to exorcise it by confronting it. Cook a green-with-envy meal, ideally serve it to the person or persons responsible for evoking such negative and wasteful feelings.

The theme of this meal is, you've guessed it, the colour green. Will it work? Of course! Imagine how your feelings will diffuse as you serve avocado soup, followed by pesto pasta with a green salad. Serve an emerald fruit salad for dessert. You might even turn the tables and have your guest or guests envious of you. If they aren't, well, at least you will have dealt with your feelings in a positive and definite way.

GREEN-EYED SOUP

SERVES 6

3 MEDIUM-SIZED RIPE AVOCADOS

2 CLOVES GARLIC, CRUSHED

JUICE OF 1 LEMON

FRESHLY GROUND BLACK PEPPER

1.35 LITRES/2 ½ PINTS/6 CUPS VEGETABLE STOCK

275 ML/10 FL OZ/1 ¼ CUPS SOURED CREAM

1 TABLESPOON SHELLED PISTACHIO NUTS, CHOPPED

BUNCH OF FRESH CHERVIL

- HALVE AVOCADOS AND **SCOOP OUT** FLESH.
- BLEND IN PROCESSOR WITH GARLIC, LEMON JUICE AND PEPPER.
- HEAT VEGETABLE STOCK UNTIL SIMMERING.
- ADD AVOCADO MIXTURE.
- WHEN HEATED THROUGH AND WELL MIXED, **ADD** SOURED CREAM.
- CONTINUE TO HEAT MIXTURE GENTLY.
- POUR INTO BOWLS AND **SPRINKLE** WITH PISTACHIO NUTS AND FRESH CHERVIL .
- SERVE.

PESTO PASTA

SERVES 6

8 TABLESPOONS FRESH PARSLEY, CHOPPED

6 TABLESPOONS FRESH BASIL, CHOPPED

4 TABLESPOONS PINE NUTS, TOASTED

110 ML/4 FL OZ/½ CUP OLIVE OIL

450 G/1 LB PASTA

GRATED PARMESAN CHEESE TO GARNISH

- **PULVERISE** HERBS AND NUTS USING MORTAR AND PESTLE.
- **PLACE** IN BOWL WITH OIL.
- **COMBINE** UNTIL SMOOTH.
- **COOK** PASTA ACCORDING TO INSTRUCTIONS ON PACK – ROUGHLY 8-10 MINUTES.
- **DRAIN** AND **TOSS** IN SAUCE.
- **SPRINKLE** WITH PARMESAN CHEESE AND **SERVE**.

EMERALD SALAD

SERVES 6

1 HONEYDEW MELON

3 KIWI FRUIT

1 TABLESPOON HONEY

½ BOTTLE OF DRY WHITE WINE

1 TABLESPOON MINT, CHOPPED

1 BUNCH GREEN SEEDLESS GRAPES

MINT SPRIGS TO GARNISH

- **SCOOP OUT** BALLS FROM MELON USING MELON BALLER.
- **PEEL** AND **SLICE** KIWI FRUIT.
- **DISSOLVE** HONEY IN WINE.
- **ADD** CHOPPED MINT TO LIQUID.
- **PLACE** MELON BALLS IN GLASS SERVING BOWL WITH KIWIS AND GRAPES.
- **POUR** LIQUID OVER FRUIT.
- **PLACE** IN FREEZER FOR 15 MINUTES.
- **ARRANGE** SPRIGS OF MINT ON TOP AND SERVE.

To drink: a white Burgundy.

EXTRAVAGANT

Everything in excess! To enjoy the flavour of life, take big bites.
Moderation is for monks.
Time Enough for Love, Robert Heinlein

There is only one problem with this mood – it has come to mean excess and waste. Needless to say I disagree wholeheartedly with this interpretation. But then I would say that, there's hardly a puritanical bone in *my* body!

A few years ago, on holiday in Italy, I decided to be extravagant and eat in a very expensive restaurant in Florence. My partner and I chose the six-course menu and set-to hungrily. At an adjoining table sat a petite Japanese gentleman, eating alone. His behaviour was distinctly odd. As each dish arrived he went into a ritual of oohing and aahing, followed by an elaborate smelling ceremony, in which he wafted the aroma of each dish under his nose by flapping his hand rapidly over it. This ritual was re-enacted for each dish and, oddest of all, the man took only one or two forkfuls of food from each dish and then sent the hardly touched plate back to the kitchen with an instruction to bring the next course out as soon as possible.

Curiosity got the better of me, and I began to chat with him. He was from Toyko and was touring the European Michelin restaurants on his own. I asked him why he sent each dish back after only one mouthful and he replied: 'Madame, I do not want to end up looking like a Westerner.' He couldn't possibly have been referring to me!

Extravagance should never be mixed with guilt. So here goes!

The minute I hear champagne mentioned, I cheer up. A smile starts at the corner of my mouth, only just though – I won't break into a full-faced grin until my glass is brimming over, and I can savour one of humankind's most celebrated drinks.

The luxurious abandon of all those little bubbles rushing to the surface of the glass reminds me of those who cock a snook at life and proclaim, 'Hey world! I don't care how much you get me down, I'm still gonna have a good time.'

This recipe has the advantage of leaving plenty of bubbly for you to fill a glass or two to the rim.

CHAMPAGNE RISOTTO

SERVES 2

4 TABLESPOONS OLIVE OIL

2 CLOVES GARLIC, CRUSHED

½ LEEK, FINELY SLICED

85 G/3 OZ/½ CUP ARBORIO RICE

225 ML/8 FL OZ/1 CUP VEGETABLE STOCK

55 G/2 OZ MIXED SHIITAKE, OYSTER AND CHANTERELLE MUSHROOMS, SLICED

6 SPEARS FRESH ASPARAGUS, CUT UP

225 ML/8 FL OZ/1 CUPS CHAMPAGNE
(OR CHEAT AND USE GOOD QUALITY SPARKLING WINE)

PARMESAN CHEESE TO GARNISH

FRESHLY GROUND BLACK PEPPER

FRESH CHIVES, CHOPPED

- HEAT OIL IN LARGE PAN.

- ADD GARLIC AND LEEK.

- STIR-FRY FOR ABOUT 6 MINUTES.

- ADD RICE AND STIR-FRY FOR ABOUT 2 MINUTES.

- ADD HALF OF VEGETABLE STOCK AND STIR OCCASIONALLY.

- WHEN ALMOST FULLY ABSORBED, ADD REST OF STOCK.

- POUR IN CHAMPAGNE AND STIR.

- COOK FOR APPROXIMATELY 15-20 MINUTES.

- SAUTÉ MUSHROOMS AND ASPARAGUS UNTIL TENDER.

- ADD IN AT THE LAST MOMENT.

- SPRINKLE WITH PARMESAN CHEESE AND BLACK PEPPER.

- GARNISH WITH CHIVES.

I learned to cook lobsters in Maine, New England. Maine is like the West of Ireland, with a rocky coastline and the cold waters of the North Atlantic producing some of the tastiest lobsters you'll find anywhere in the world. I've been there a few times. I rent a clapboard shack on Gooserocks Beach, near Kennebunkport. I usually go there in early summer, before the high season, when everything is open but prices haven't yet skyrocketed.

Lobster is a fast food in Maine. Trailers on the side of the road sell – wait for it – lobster rolls, fresh, steamed and served with a piquant sauce in a crusty breadroll. Eaten at a wooden picnic bench on the roadside with a chilled bottle of beer you couldn't imagine a more delicious and unpretentious, or unextravagant, snack. I adore the simplicity of it all. Only in America could such a premium food be turned into a fast food.

In Ireland, lobster has been given the status of a superfood for the wealthy or the extravagant. It brings tears to my eyes, because lobster could be just as easily available and as cheap in Ireland as it is in Maine. But instead Irish lobster is exported to the gastronomic centres of mainland Europe.

Anyway, during my visits to Maine I developed an affinity for our crustacean friends and learnt that the very, very best way to eat lobster is the simplest way of all: boil it, crack it open, and consume it by dipping morsels in lime butter. Wash down that beauty with bread and salad, and a glass of chilled white wine or a cold beer.

But how do you actually cook that critter?

Some people get very squeamish and baulk at the thought of the lobsters being scalded to death, emitting that supposed high-pitched scream. Believe me, this does not happen. The lobsters die instantly. Any twitches are just the nerve ends pulsating.

Equipment for cooking: large pot and lots of nerve.
- Heat enough water in a large pot to cover lobsters
- Drop in lobsters when water boils
- Simmer for approximately 10 minutes – lobsters will turn bright red

Equipment for eating: All you need is a narrow fork, a shell cracker, a big napkin to stop splashes getting on your clothes, determination and a fingerbowl.

Here is how to crack open a lobster the Maine way:
- Cover boiled lobster with napkin to avoid scalding hands
- Lift entire lobster, with head in your left hand and tail in your right
- Snap off tail with a firm movement, as if you were breaking bread

- Hold tail in your left hand and snap off splayed fin at end
- Take fork and shove it with a firm movement up lobster's bum, where splayed fin was
- Lo and behold, entire tail-meat section will pop out intact
- Put claws in dishcloth and bash a few times with small hammer or similar object
- Pick out meat using appropriate cutlery

Now for the recipes:

LOBSTER 'N' LIME

SERVES 2

ONE 650 G/1 ½ LB LOBSTER

4 TABLESPOONS BUTTER

JUICE OF 1 LIME

- **BOIL** LOBSTER FOR 10 MINUTES.
- **MELT** BUTTER IN PAN.
- **ADD** LIME JUICE.
- **SERVE** LOBSTER ON PLATE.
- **SERVE** LIME SAUCE IN SMALL BOWL.
- **SET** EMPTY BOWL ON STANDBY FOR SHELL BITS AND GENERAL DEBRIS.
- **SET** BOWL FILLED WITH WATER FOR FINGER RINSING ALONGSIDE.

OTT Pudding

Serves 2

55 G/2 OZ DARK CHOCOLATE

1 TABLESPOON STRONG HOT COFFEE

2 FREE RANGE EGGS

½ MANGO

JUICE OF 1 LIME

1 TABLESPOON GRATED DARK CHOCOLATE, TO GARNISH

SPRIG OF MINT TO GARNISH

- **BREAK UP** CHOCOLATE INTO SQUARES.
- **PLACE** IN BOWL OVER SAUCEPAN OF BARELY SIMMERING WATER.
- **MELT** SLOWLY.
- **ADD** HOT COFFEE.
- **STIR** WELL.
- **REMOVE** FROM HEAT.
- **SEPARATE** EGGS.
- **BEAT** YOLKS INTO CHOCOLATE.
- **WHISK** WHITES UNTIL STIFF.
- **FOLD** WHITES GENTLY INTO CHOCOLATE.
- **POUR** INTO PRETTY GLASSES.
- **CHILL** FOR 2 HOURS.
- **SCOOP OUT** FLESH OF MANGO.
- **BLEND** WITH LIME JUICE.
- **SIEVE** MIXTURE.
- **POUR** OVER MOUSSE IN GLASSES.
- **SPRINKLE** WITH GRATED CHOCOLATE.
- **SERVE** WITH SPRIG OF MINT ON TOP.

F E D   U P

Repeat this phrase: My body is a temple.

Hard to believe if you're having a fat day. Self-abuse – the calorific kind – the wrong kind of food, the one last drink for the road, that spicy dish, the chocolate *bombe* that couldn't be resisted – all can make you feel, literally, fed up. Our bodies have to work so hard at gulping, digesting and transporting all the food and drink we shovel in that it's important to give them the occasional day off. The best possible way to combat the fat slug feeling is to hit the juice trail. Plan it for a Saturday or Sunday or, if you have a will of iron, the whole weekend so you don't have to contend with the stresses and temptations of your work schedule.

Ease up on food on Friday, no red meat, no pastries, biscuits, white breads or dairy products. Instead eat lots of fruit and veg. Try miso soup for lunch with a light salad. Drink lots of water and stock up on healthy supplies for your clean-out day.

Choose two different types of fruit, one for the morning and one for the rest of the day – oranges and melons, apples and pink grapefruit, or grapes and pears. Buy in your favourite herbal teas and fruit juices – you're going to drink eight pints of water during the day. But don't mix the water and fruit juices, it's better for your digestion not to dilute the juice. This is a time-out day, make sure you've nothing planned, just let your system rest.

- Wake up with a glass of warm water (boiled and cooling) with a squeeze of fresh orange or lemon juice to flush those toxins out

- For breakfast, juice up your chosen fruit and drink one or two glasses

- Mid-morning, try some herbal tea

- Lunch is another glass or two of juiced fruit

- Early evening, yes, another juice drink

- And finally, take a soothing herbal tea, chamomile, or rosehip, to bed with you

Remember, if you have any doubts about your state of health, check with your doctor before you embark on a clean-out. Whether you're following this DIY colonic irrigation diet for one day or two, re-introduce real food gently afterwards – no beef burgers and beer. Stick to yoghurt, salads and clear soups, and energy-giving fruits like bananas.

G R A T E F U L

Personally, I think if a woman hasn't met the right man by the time she's twenty-four, she may be lucky.
Deborah Kerr

I know it's a cliché (well, two clichés actually) but you've gotta accentuate the positive, or, be thankful for small mercies. It's the key to happiness, especially when life seems to have handed you a rough deal. Why should you feel grateful? Well, just think about it. Make a list of the top five reasons why, if you must. It'll give you some perspective on your life, and day-to-day hassles and disappointments will lose their power over you.

Then again, you may have someone you want to thank. A friend who stood by you through the upheaval of a relationship break-up. My experience is that there is nothing more pleasurable than someone cooking you a Thanksgiving meal. It is really a two or three hour indulgence feast where the mantra of 'Thank You' is repeated in every dish, every item of food, every minute spent in preparation.

That is, of course, if the food is edible.

If the food is awful then you might be led to believe that your host is really giving you entirely another message! I was once served yoghurt and lettuce soup in a friend's house. It was easily the most disgusting green slop I have ever had to endure. My partner covered up for my lack of appetite by announcing gallantly: 'The soup's great, I'll have another bowl!' I continued the charade of having no appetite and hours later I drove home, starving, wondering how my friend could possibly have cooked up food that tasted so awful!

The point is, get the menu right and get a feel for food. What follows is an alternative Thanksgiving menu for four.

But first, a welcoming drink: the famous Bellini cocktail which was invented in Harry's Bar and Grill in Venice. I drank one there once and thought it the most delicious and refreshing pre-dinner drink. Back home I discovered to my delight that my home-made Bellini tasted just as good and, importantly, was a whole lot cheaper!

THE WELCOME DRINK

SERVES 4

2 PEACHES, PEELED AND HALVED

1 BOTTLE GOOD QUALITY SPARKLING WINE OR CHAMPAGNE

- **PURÉE** PEACHES.
- **POUR** CHAMPAGNE INTO EACH GLASS.
- **ADD** TABLESPOON OF PURÉE TO EACH GLASS.
- **SIP.**

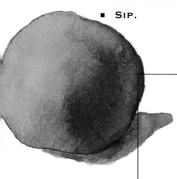

SURPRISE PARCELS

SERVES 4

1 MEDIUM LEEK

5 TABLESPOONS OLIVE OIL

3 SHEETS FILO PASTRY

350 G/12 OZ FETA CHEESE, CUBED

2 TABLESPOONS MELTED BUTTER

- **PRE-HEAT** OVEN TO 200°C/400°F/GAS MARK 6.
- **SLICE** LEEKS INTO SMALL STRIPS.
- **SWEAT** IN OLIVE OIL OVER LOW HEAT FOR 10 MINUTES.
- **CUT** EACH PASTRY SHEET INTO 4 AND **BRUSH** WITH OLIVE OIL.
- **PLACE** ON OILED BAKING SHEET.
- **PLACE** CUBED CHEESE IN MIDDLE OF EACH SQUARE, 25 G/1 OZ FOR EACH PARCEL.
- **PLACE** LEEKS ALONGSIDE CHEESE IN FILO PASTRY.
- **PICK UP** CORNERS AND, WITH WET FINGERS, **GATHER** PARCELS TOGETHER AT TOPS AND **GLAZE** WITH MELTED BUTTER.
- **BAKE** FOR 15 MINUTES.
- **SERVE** WITH DELIGHT.

CELEBRATION LAMB

SERVES 4

2 RACKS OF LAMB (6 RIBS PER RACK)

4 TABLESPOONS OLIVE OIL

4 CLOVES GARLIC

4 SPRIGS FRESH ROSEMARY

FRESHLY GROUND BLACK PEPPER

PINCH OF SEA SALT

- **PRE-HEAT** OVEN TO 200°C/400°F/GAS MARK 6.
- **DIVIDE** EACH RACK IN HALF.
- **BRUSH** EACH RACK WITH OLIVE OIL.
- **PLACE** GARLIC CLOVES AND ROSEMARY UNDER MEAT IN A ROASTING TIN.
- **SPRINKLE** WITH SEA SALT AND PEPPER.
- **ROAST** FOR 20 MINUTES (SHOULD BE SLIGHTLY PINK).
- **SERVE** WITH ROAST VEGETABLES.

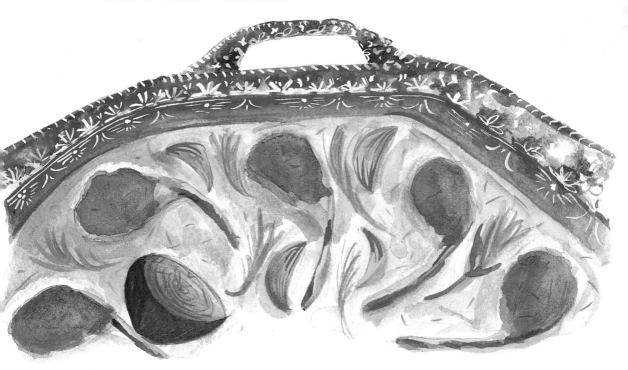

ROAST VEGETABLES

SERVES 4

1/2 MEDIUM CAULIFLOWER

2 PARSNIPS

4 SMALL ONIONS

4 CLOVES GARLIC, UNPEELED

2 TABLESPOONS OLIVE OIL

- **BREAK** CAULIFLOWER INTO SMALL FLORETS.
- **PEEL** AND **CHOP** PARSNIP INTO BITE-SIZED PIECES.
- **TOP** AND **TAIL** ONIONS BUT **LEAVE** SKIN ON.
- **PLACE** GARLIC ON BAKING SHEET ALONG WITH OTHER VEGETABLES.
- **SPRINKLE** OLIVE OIL OVER VEGETABLES.
- **PLACE** IN OVEN WITH LAMB FOR ABOUT 30 MINUTES.
- **SERVE.**

PORTLY PRUNES

SERVES 4

20 LARGE PRUNES, DRIED

1/2 BOTTLE REASONABLE QUALITY PORT

ZEST AND JUICE OF SMALL LEMON

1/2 TEASPOON CINNAMON

PINCH GROUND CLOVES

170 ML/6 FL OZ/3/4 CUP WATER

3 TABLESPOONS FLAKED ALMONDS, TOASTED

- **RINSE** PRUNES.
- **PLACE** WITH PORT IN DEEP BOWL, **COVER** AND **SOAK** FOR 3 HOURS.
- **PUT** PRUNES AND PORT IN SAUCEPAN.
- **ADD** GRATED ZEST AND JUICE OF LEMON, CINNAMON, CLOVES AND WATER.
- **SIMMER** FOR 10 MINUTES — **DO NOT OVERCOOK** OR PRUNES TURN TO MUSH.
- **PLACE** IN INDIVIDUAL SERVING GLASSES AND **CHILL.**
- **SPRINKLE** WITH TOASTED ALMONDS BEFORE SERVING.

To drink: a good red Rioja, at least of Reserva quality. A Gran Reserva if you're feeling very grateful

GUILTY

Show me the woman who doesn't feel guilty and I'll show you a man.
Erica Jong

This is the most useless emotion known to humanity. We feel guilty about things we haven't done. Guilty about the things we have done. Real guilt-trippers even feel guilty about feeling guilty! I say dump it. That's right, gather the whole useless emotion in a lump, open the window wide and throw it out.

Easier said than done, I know. And one of the biggest sources of guilt for any woman is food. Every time I look at 'Baywatch' or read a glossy magazine I think that to be the perfect desirable woman I must be no less than a wizened size 12. I'm not: I feel guilty. I eat a cream cake: I feel guilty. In fact, guilt and food are partners in a horrible cycle.

The key is moderation. There is nothing wrong with eating sweet things. It's only if it gets out of control that the trouble starts. And then the cycle begins – you over-eat; then you feel guilty so you diet; you're starving and feeling deprived, so you become obsessed with food; so you end up over-eating again. No, I believe in the No Diet diet – eat a little (and every now and then you can eat a lot!) of whatever you like, and enjoy it. Without guilt.

Here is a dessert to send you into orbit.

GUILT-FREE CHOCOLATE CREAM

SERVES 1

175 G/6 OZ PLAIN DARK CHOCOLATE (70% COCOA SOLIDS)
225 ML/8 FL OZ/1 CUP SINGLE CREAM
1 MEDIUM FREE RANGE EGG
VANILLA ESSENCE
80 ML/2 ½ FL OZ/⅓ CUP COGNAC

- **BREAK UP** CHOCOLATE AND **PUT** IN PROCESSOR.
- **HEAT** CREAM GENTLY AND **POUR** INTO CHOCOLATE.
- **BLEND** UNTIL SMOOTH.
- **ADD** HALF BEATEN EGG AND A FEW DROPS OF VANILLA ESSENCE.
- **WHIZZ** AGAIN.
- **ADD** REST OF EGG.
- **WHIZZ** ONCE MORE.
- **DIVIDE** CHOCOLATE MIXTURE INTO INDIVIDUAL GLASSES.
- **POUR** SPOONFUL OF COGNAC OVER EACH SERVING.
- **SAVOUR.**

HAPPY

Happiness is good health and a bad memory.
Ingrid Bergman

This has to be everyone's favourite mood. People chase it all their lives. Some try to buy it, others try to find it through drink, drugs, sex or God. But to be happy is an occasional gift. And when it appears it should be prolonged and celebrated.

To me it is a mood of bright colours, sunlight and the evocative aromas of my happiest times – those sun-drenched holidays abroad. If happiness were a place for me it would have to be a quiet Mediterranean fishing village, with white-washed houses and olive groves and orange and lemon trees stretching into the distance.

If it were food it would have to be paella.

But let's begin with a starter, a traditional Spanish soup: the famous cold Gazpacho. Not only is it zesty and tangy, but it looks great – and is wonderfully cool on a hot summer's day.

GAZPACHO

SERVES 4

450 G/1 LB RIPE TOMATOES

1 MEDIUM ONION

1 MEDIUM RED BELL PEPPER

$\frac{1}{2}$ CUCUMBER, CHOPPED

JUICE OF 2 LIMES

2 CLOVES GARLIC, CRUSHED

570 ML/1 PINT/$2\frac{1}{2}$ CUPS VEGETABLE STOCK

2 TABLESPOONS TOMATO PURÉE

2 TABLESPOONS OLIVE OIL

FRESHLY GROUND BLACK PEPPER

PINCH OF SEA SALT

TABASCO SAUCE TO TASTE

1 GREEN PEPPER, CHOPPED, TO GARNISH

BUNCH OF FRESH BASIL

- **IMMERSE** TOMATOES IN BOILING WATER.
- **WAIT** FOR 30 SECONDS.
- **TRANSFER** TO COOL WATER AND **PEEL** SKINS.
- **HALVE** TOMATOES AND **DE-SEED.**
- **BLEND** TOMATOES ALONG WITH ROUGHLY CHOPPED ONION, RED PEPPER, CUCUMBER, LIME JUICE AND GARLIC CLOVES.
- **ADD** COOLED VEGETABLE STOCK AND TOMATO PURÉE.
- **ADD** PEPPER AND TABASCO SAUCE TO TASTE.
- **COVER** AND **CHILL** FOR ONE HOUR.
- **GARNISH** WITH GREEN PEPPER AND BASIL.
- **SERVE.**

This dish looks spectacular and is great for a dinner party. It's Spain's best-known dish and is named from the Catalan word for 'skillet', the metal cooking pot.

PARADISICAL PAELLA

SERVES 4

2 TABLESPOONS OIL

1 LARGE ONION, CHOPPED

3 CLOVES GARLIC, CHOPPED

1 RED PEPPER

175 G/6 OZ CHICKEN MEAT

2-3 MEDIUM TOMATOES, PEELED AND CHOPPED

350 G/12 OZ/2 CUPS LONG GRAIN RICE

1 TEASPOON SAFFRON THREADS

1 LITRE/1¾ PINTS/4 CUPS VEGETABLE STOCK

450 G/1 LB MUSSELS IN THEIR SHELLS

450 G/1 LB CLAMS IN THEIR SHELLS

225 G/8 OZ PRAWNS IN THEIR SHELLS

275 ML/10 FL OZ/1¼ CUPS CREAM (OPTIONAL)

FRESHLY GROUND BLACK PEPPER

PINCH OF SEA SALT

WEDGES OF LEMON TO GARNISH

- **PRE-HEAT** OVEN TO 180°C/350°F/GAS MARK 4.
- **HEAT** OIL IN PAN OVER HIGH HEAT.
- **SAUTÉ** ONION, GARLIC AND PEPPER.
- **ADD** CHICKEN MEAT.
- **LOWER** HEAT AND **BROWN** CHICKEN.
- **ADD** PEELED AND CHOPPED TOMATOES.
- **STIR** IN RICE AND SAFFRON.
- **ADD** STOCK.
- **CONTINUE TO SIMMER**, AND **STIR** FOR 30 MINUTES.
- **SCRUB** AND **WASH** MUSSELS AND CLAMS THOROUGHLY.
- **DISCARD** SHELLS THAT ARE SLIGHTLY OPEN.
- **RINSE** PRAWNS IN WATER.
- **PLACE** RICE IN OVENPROOF BOWL.
- **ARRANGE** SHELLFISH IN RICE.

- **PLACE** IN OVEN FOR 10 MINUTES.

- **DISCARD** ANY SHELLFISH THAT HAVE NOT OPENED.

- **STIR** IN CREAM FOR A RICHER SAUCE.

- **ADD** BLACK PEPPER AND SEA SALT.

- **SERVE** WITH WEDGES OF LEMON.

NECTARINA NIRVANA

SERVES 4

2 LARGE NECTARINES OR PEACHES

JUICE OF 1 LEMON

2 ORANGES

1 TEASPOON ORANGE ZEST

1 GLASS COINTREAU

1 FREE RANGE EGG

- **PEEL** AND **DE-STONE** FRUIT.

- **BLEND** ALL INGREDIENTS.

- **SERVE** OVER CRUSHED ICE.

To drink: a white Rioja

H A T E

There is a finality about hating something or somebody. I mean, how much worse can it get?

I was once told of a hate tale involving a person of high office, someone who over the years had attracted his fair share of hate vibes.

He happened to be away from home one evening and decided to have dinner in a hotel in the country. He and his entourage settled in for the evening, assembled in the restaurant and placed their orders. This person chose steak.

Unbeknownst to him there happened to be a chef in the kitchen who, for some reason lost in the mists of time, harboured a deep and abiding hatred for him.

This chef took the victim's order for steak, went over to the meat locker and selected a juicy specimen. He walked to a small hatch overlooking the restaurant and stared at the object of his hatred. Taking the steak in his hands he rubbed it up and down against his genitalia a few times, and then cooked it.

The well-seasoned steak went out to the customer and the chef settled down to watch at the serving hatch, while the unsuspecting man devoured the meat with gusto.

The moral of the story, for me anyway, is twofold.

First, try not to end up with someone hating you.

Second, if someone *is* going to hate you, make sure it is not a chef who is just about to serve you food.

That's why I have a policy of never complaining in restaurants before the last course is served. You just never know.

Controlled hatred, on the other hand, can be fun. Take, for example, an ex-husband or partner who you feel has done the dirty on you. Invite him to dinner and the taste experience of a lifetime. Reel him in by telling him you've arranged a bevy of beauties to meet him.

No man would ever be this naive, I hear you say.

Folks, you're wrong. This menu is inspired by a true incident, no urban myths here.

Start with a soup which will lull him into a false sense of security.

CUNNING CORN CHOWDER

SERVES 4

1 TABLESPOON OIL

1 MEDIUM ONION, CHOPPED

8 EARS OF CORN (IF FRESH CORN NOT AVAILABLE USE FROZEN)

850 ML/1½ PINTS/3½ CUPS VEGETABLE STOCK

1 RED PEPPER, CHOPPED

1-2 TEASPOONS FRESH ROSEMARY, CHOPPED

1-2 TEASPOONS DRIED THYME

FRESHLY GROUND BLACK PEPPER

1 TABLESPOON FRESH CHIVES, CHOPPED

CAYENNE PEPPER FOR SPECIAL GUEST

- HEAT OIL IN LARGE SAUCEPAN OVER MEDIUM HEAT FOR ABOUT 1 MINUTE.

- SAUTÉ ONION UNTIL TRANSLUCENT, ABOUT 5 MINUTES.

- SHEAR CORN OFF 8 COBS – SLIDING A SHARP KNIFE UP AND DOWN COB TO REMOVE CORN.

- SAUTÉ FOR 4 TO 5 MINUTES.

- ADD VEGETABLE STOCK.

- COOK UNTIL CORN IS SOFT AND CAN BE SQUISHED UNDER A FORK.

- WHIZZ CONTENTS OF PAN IN PROCESSOR UNTIL SMOOTH.

- POUR BACK INTO PAN.

- ADD RED PEPPER, ROSEMARY, THYME, PEPPER, CAYENNE AND REST OF VEGETABLE STOCK AND CORN.

- STIR FOR ANOTHER 10 TO 15 MINUTES, UNTIL THICK AND CREAMY.

- GARNISH WITH CHOPPED CHIVES.

- NB: BEFORE SERVING, ISOLATE SOUP FOR THE EX-BELOVED AND LACE HELPING WITH CAYENNE PEPPER – JUST ENOUGH TO HEAT THINGS UP TO AN UNCOMFORTABLE LEVEL.

The beauty of this hate treatment is that your victim will be completely perplexed by the cooking compliments your guests are throwing your way. Your victim will just have to struggle on and munch through the horror of it all. The next course is where you're really going to put the boot in.

LAMB BURGERS

MAKES 8
450 G/1 LB MINCED LAMB
1 ONION, FINELY CHOPPED
1 FREE RANGE EGG
FRESHLY GROUND BLACK PEPPER

- **MIX** MEAT WITH ONION IN LARGE BOWL.
- **ADD** EGG AND PEPPER.
- **MIX** WELL.
- **SHAPE** INTO BURGER-SIZED ROUNDS.
- **HEAT** OLIVE OIL.
- **SHALLOW FRY.**
- **SERVE** DROWNING IN WILD MUSHROOM SAUCE.

WILD MUSHROOM SAUCE

SERVES 4
50 G/2 OZ DRIED WILD MUSHROOMS
2 TABLESPOONS CREAM
FRESHLY GROUND BLACK PEPPER

- **POUR** ENOUGH BOILING WATER OVER MUSHROOMS TO COVER.
- **SOAK** FOR 15 MINUTES.
- **HEAT** PAN.
- **POUR** MUSHROOMS AND WATER INTO PAN.
- **BRING** TO BOIL.
- **SIMMER** TO REDUCE LIQUID UNTIL THICKENED.
- **WHIZZ** IN PROCESSOR UNTIL MUSHROOMS ARE MINCED.
- **RETURN** TO PAN.
- **ADD** CREAM AND PEPPER.
- **REDUCE** FOR 2 MINUTES.
- **PLACE** LADLEFUL OF SAUCE IN SEPARATE SAUCEPAN.
- **SEASON** THIS PORTION OF SAUCE SO THAT IT IS INEDIBLE — SALT, NUMEROUS SHAKES OF TABASCO, ETC.
- **GIVE** ONLY ONE PERSON THE SPECIAL SAUCE, GUESS WHO!

And for dessert, well, what a sweet treat you have in store!

STICKY HONEY CREAM

SERVES 4

4 FREE RANGE EGGS

6 TABLESPOONS RUNNY HONEY

170 ML/6 FL OZ/¾ CUPS CREAM

- **SEPARATE** YOLKS AND WHITES OF EGGS.
- **BEAT** YOLKS IN BOWL OVER BOILING WATER.
- SLOWLY **ADD** HONEY, BEATING CONSTANTLY.
- **TAKE** BOWL OFF BOILING WATER AND **COOL.**
- **WHISK** EGG WHITES UNTIL STIFF.
- **FOLD** EGG WHITES INTO COLD MIXTURE.
- **WHIP** CREAM AND **WHISK** INTO MIXTURE.
- **CHILL.**
- BEFORE SERVING, **TAKE** VICTIM'S PORTION AND **LASH ON** EXTRA AMOUNTS OF HONEY.
- **SERVE** HIS EXTRA-SWEET DISH ALONGSIDE EVERYONE ELSE'S AND **WATCH** YOUR VICTIM SQUIRM.

There will be a number of possibilities running through his head at the conclusion of his culinary adventure:

1 'My taste buds are losing it'

2 'What a crap cook'

3 'The other guests are mad'

4 The one thought you're hoping will plant itself in his pee wee brain: 'I'm going mad'

5 The very, very last thought to occur to him will be 'This bitch is out to get me'

Needless to say it's very important that you don't laugh out of context.

Don't you just love to hate those who deserve it?

To drink: a white Rioja

HURT

A thick skin is a gift from God.
Konrad Adenauer

I've never met anybody who didn't have the capacity to be hurt. No matter how insensitive they might appear. When you are hurt you often misinterpret the reason that motivated your attacker. 'She doesn't like me,' or 'What did I do wrong?' you think.

However, the surprising truth is that most times the reason the person is lashing out has nothing to do with you at all. That person is just plain unhappy and you are a convenient dumping ground. This doesn't stop you from feeling hurt, of course.

New Age guru and philosopher Deepak Chopra says that it is the ego which gets mauled when someone attacks you. What you need to do is detach yourself from your ego so that the real you is beyond being hurt. I suppose this is where the phrase 'Don't take it personally' comes from. It's good advice to heed.

Anyway, this is easier said than done, but when you adjust your thinking and depersonalise the attack, it is amazing how actions and comments lose their stinging power. Just deflect that missile and move on. And comfort yourself with some good earthy soup.

BROWN LENTIL SOUP

SERVES 4

110 G/4 OZ/$\frac{1}{2}$ CUP BROWN LENTILS

1 TABLESPOON OIL

1 ONION, CHOPPED

850 ML/1$\frac{1}{2}$ PINT/3$\frac{1}{2}$ CUPS VEGETABLE STOCK

2 CLOVES GARLIC, CRUSHED

DOLLOP OF CRÈME FRAÎCHE

225 ML/8 FL OZ/1 CUP WATER

ROASTED RED PEPPER STRIPS (SEE GRATEFUL)

- WASH LENTILS (THERE'S NO NEED TO SOAK THEM).
- HEAT OIL IN PAN.
- SAUTÉ ONION AND GARLIC.
- ADD VEGETABLE STOCK AND LENTILS.
- SIMMER FOR 30 MINUTES.
- DO NOT LET MIXTURE DRY OUT, KEEP IT TOPPED UP WITH WATER.
- PURÉE MIXTURE.
- RETURN TO PAN.
- ADD ENOUGH WATER TO MAKE A THICK LIQUID.
- SERVE IN BOWLS.
- GARNISH WITH DOLLOP OF CRÈME FRAÎCHE AND STRIPS OF PEELED ROASTED RED PEPPER.

CHICKEN RISOTTO

SERVES 4

2 TABLESPOONS BUTTER

1 ONION, CHOPPED

$\frac{1}{2}$ RED PEPPER, FINELY CHOPPED

115 G/4 OZ CHICKEN MEAT

225 G/8 OZ/1 $\frac{1}{4}$ CUPS ARBORIO RICE

1.2 LITRES/2 PINTS/5 CUPS CHICKEN STOCK

A FEW THREADS OF SAFFRON

FRESHLY GROUND BLACK PEPPER

55 G/2 OZ PARMESAN CHEESE, GRATED

PARMESAN SHAVINGS FOR GARNISH

- MELT BUTTER IN LARGE SAUCEPAN.
- ADD ONION.
- COOK FOR 5 MINUTES UNTIL SOFT.
- ADD FINELY CHOPPED RED PEPPER AND CHICKEN PIECES.
- ADD RICE.
- STIR IN SLOWLY TO COAT GRAINS IN BUTTER.
- COOK FOR 1 MINUTE.
- ADD 4 TABLESPOONS CHICKEN STOCK.
- COOK UNTIL STOCK HAS BEEN ABSORBED.
- ADD SAFFRON AND BLACK PEPPER.
- CONTINUE TO ADD STOCK UNTIL RISOTTO IS THICK AND CREAMY AND RICE IS TENDER.
- COOK FOR 20 TO 25 MINUTES.
- STIR IN REMAINING BUTTER AND PARMESAN.
- TOP WITH PARMESAN SHAVINGS.
- SERVE IMMEDIATELY.

NOODLES WITH POPPY SEEDS

SERVES 4

4 TABLESPOONS POPPY SEEDS

200 ML/7 FL OZ/1 SCANT ($\frac{7}{8}$) CUP MILK

3 TABLESPOONS HONEY

110 ML/4 FL OZ/$\frac{1}{2}$ CUP CREAM

1 TEASPOON LEMON ZEST

1 TEASPOON VANILLA EXTRACT

85 G/3 OZ ALMONDS, CHOPPED COARSELY

450 G/1 LB NOODLES, MEDIUM SIZED

- **GRIND** POPPY SEEDS IN PESTLE AND MORTAR.

- **SOAK** IN MILK FOR 2 HOURS.

- **DRAIN.**

- **COMBINE** HONEY, CREAM, LEMON ZEST AND GROUND POPPY SEEDS IN SAUCEPAN.

- **COOK** OVER LOW HEAT, STIRRING FREQUENTLY UNTIL THICK.

- **STIR** IN VANILLA AND ALMONDS AND **KEEP WARM.**

- **SIMMER** NOODLES IN BOILING WATER FOR 2 MINUTES.

- **TOSS** NOODLES IN SAUCE.

- **SERVE** WARM.

INDULGENT

The only way to rid yourself of temptation is to yield to it.
Oscar Wilde

You're pregnant! Honey, you deserve to be indulged. Rule one for this mood is that you are *not* to cook. Neither are you to help in the preparation or cleaning up.

If necessary, have the cooking instructions written out in clear legible writing and ask your guest to be confident and get on with the job.

And just who should this guest be? Who is your favourite person? Who do you feel most comfortable with? Who makes you smile?

It doesn't have to be your current partner (though it's food for thought if it isn't), it could be an old friend or an old flame. It could be somebody you only like in small doses.

Think about this carefully and then ask this person along to do the cooking for you and share the results.

Plan the following:
- Ensure that the ingredients and cooking utensils are easy to find
- Organise it so that you should be eating by 8 pm
- At 6 pm, draw a bath and add plenty of oils and salts
- Check the oils carefully – some should not be used during pregnancy
- Switch off the lights and light some aromatherapy candles
- Play some relaxing music
- Pour yourself a freshly squeezed fruit juice, and climb into the bath
- Soak for 20 minutes
- Wrap yourself in a very large towel and, having arranged the masseur beforehand, proceed to the room where he/she has set up
- This room should be warm, lit by candles, and the same music should be playing.
- Relax and be massaged for 1 hour

In the meantime your special guest will be preparing you a feast. The ingredients of these dishes will indulge your mood – carbohydrates and cream slow the body down, while lettuce induces sleep.

NB: Try to stay awake while eating.

CREAMY PEA SOUP

SERVES 2

1 TABLESPOON OLIVE OIL

1 SMALL ONION, FINELY CHOPPED

4 LARGE LETTUCE LEAVES (BUTTERHEAD OR SIMILAR), CHOPPED

200 G/7 OZ /2 CUPS PEAS, SHELLED

570 ML/1 PINT/2$\frac{1}{2}$ CUPS VEGETABLE STOCK

110 ML/4 FL OZ/$\frac{1}{2}$ CUP CRÈME FRAÎCHE

FRESHLY GROUND BLACK PEPPER

SPRIG OF TARRAGON

- **HEAT** OIL IN PAN.
- **SAUTÉ** ONION.
- **ADD** CHOPPED LETTUCE.
- **STIR** FOR 30 SECONDS.
- **ADD** PEAS.
- **STIR** IN STOCK.
- **BRING** TO BOIL.
- **SIMMER** FOR 20 MINUTES.
- **PURÉE** SOUP.
- **RETURN** TO SAUCEPAN.
- **REHEAT** GENTLY.
- **ADD** CRÈME FRAÎCHE.
- **BLEND** THOROUGHLY.
- **ADD** PEPPER.
- **SERVE** WITH SPRIG OF TARRAGON.

SMOKED SALMON PASTA

SERVES 2

1 TABLESPOON OLIVE OIL

PINCH OF SALT

225 G/8 OZ TAGLIATELLE

55 G/2 OZ SMOKED SALMON

1 ONION, FINELY CHOPPED

2 CLOVES GARLIC, CRUSHED

110 ML/4 FL OZ /$\frac{1}{2}$ CUP DOUBLE CREAM

2 TEASPOONS PINK PEPPERCORNS

FRESHLY GROUND BLACK PEPPER

2 TABLESPOONS CHOPPED CHIVES

- **BRING** A LARGE SAUCEPAN OF WATER TO THE BOIL.
- **ADD** DROP OF OLIVE OIL AND PINCH OF SALT.
- **COOK** PASTA UNTIL AL DENTE.
- **CUT** SALMON INTO STRIPS.
- **HEAT** OLIVE OIL IN FRYING-PAN.
- **SAUTÉ** ONION AND GARLIC.
- AFTER 1 MINUTE, **POUR** CREAM INTO PAN OVER GARLIC AND ONIONS.
- **REDUCE** CREAM OVER HIGH HEAT.
- **ADD** PINK PEPPERCORNS.
- **STIR** FOR 2 MINUTES.
- **ADD** STRIPS OF SALMON.
- **DRAIN** PASTA.
- **COMBINE** PASTA AND SAUCE.
- **ADD** PEPPER TO TASTE.
- **SERVE** WITH SPRINKLE OF CHIVES ON TOP.

HOT FRUIT COMPOTE

SERVES 2

115 G/4 OZ MIXED DRIED FRUITS,
PEARS, APPLES, PRUNES, RAISINS

JUICE OF 2 ORANGES

1 CINNAMON STICK

ZEST OF 1 ORANGE

110 ML/4 FL OZ/$\frac{1}{2}$ CUP COINTREAU

SMALL CARTON NATURAL YOGHURT

- **HEAT** FRUIT IN PAN WITH ORANGE JUICE AND CINNAMON STICK.
- **BRING** TO BOIL.
- **SIMMER** FOR 2 MINUTES.
- **REMOVE** FROM HEAT.
- **ADD** ORANGE ZEST AND COINTREAU.
- **SOAK** OVERNIGHT.
- WHEN NEEDED, **HEAT** THROUGH.
- **SERVE** WITH CHILLED YOGHURT.

To drink: a good Cabernet Sauvignon

J O V I A L

Never keep up with the Joneses.
Drag them down to your level – it's cheaper.
Quentin Crisp

Recently I heard a journalist ask a chef what she and her sister talked about when working in the kitchen of their restaurant and the bald answer came back: 'Nothing'. I don't know why, but food in all its shapes and forms has always been taken far too seriously. Yes, food deserves to be taken seriously, but really! The almost complete absence of humour is strange and unnecessary. Think about the amount of fun people have during eating!

I hope the recipes here demonstrate that it is possible to enjoy your food and encourage a sense of humour, all at the same time. Nothing is as it seems, especially with the following recipe – a mushroom soup that looks like a frothy cappuccino – which leaves guests wondering: 'Has she gone mad and started with dessert?'

MUSHROOM CAPPUCCINO

SERVES 4

2 TABLESPOONS BUTTER

350 G/12 OZ MUSHROOMS, SLICED

570 ML/1 PINT/2½ CUPS VEGETABLE STOCK

1 MEDIUM POTATO, PEELED AND DICED

140 ML/5 FL OZ/⅔ CUP MILK

140 ML/5 FL OZ/⅔ CUP SINGLE CREAM

FRESHLY GROUND BLACK PEPPER

ROASTED HAZELNUTS TO GARNISH

- **MELT** BUTTER IN PAN.
- **ADD** SLICED MUSHROOMS TO PAN.
- **SAUTÉ** FOR ABOUT 2-3 MINUTES.
- **ADD** VEGETABLE STOCK AND POTATO.
- **SIMMER** FOR ANOTHER 20 MINUTES.
- **PURÉE.**
- **PUT** BACK IN POT ON HEAT.
- **ADD** MILK AND CREAM.
- **BRING** TO BOIL.
- **ADD** PEPPER.
- **TAKE** 2 TABLESPOONS OF SOUP AND **ADD** 2 TABLESPOONS OF WATER.
- **WHISK** WITH A HAND-HELD BLENDER UNTIL FOAMING.
- **DIVIDE** REMAINDER OF SOUP INTO COFFEE CUPS.
- **SPOON** TABLESPOON OF FROTH ON TOP OF EACH COFFEE CUP.
- **RUB** HAZELNUTS TOGETHER GENTLY TO LOOSEN SKINS.
- **CRUSH.**
- **SPRINKLE** HAZELNUTS ON TOP TO MIMIC POWDERED COCOA.

LETTUCE EAT CHICKEN

SERVES 4

4 FREE RANGE CHICKEN BREASTS, SKINLESS

4 TABLESPOONS SOFT GOAT'S CHEESE

4 BUTTERHEAD OR OTHER SOFT LETTUCE LEAVES

1 MEDIUM RED PEPPER, CUT IN STRIPS

8 SPRING ONIONS, CHOPPED

1 TABLESPOON CHOPPED CHERVIL OR CHIVES

JUICE OF 2 LIMES

FRESHLY GROUND BLACK PEPPER

- **CUT** A SLIT DOWN THE SIDE OF EACH CHICKEN BREAST.
- **INSERT** ONE TABLESPOON GOAT'S CHEESE INTO EACH OPENING.
- **PLACE** A CHICKEN BREAST ON EACH LETTUCE LEAF.
- **ADD** SOME OF THE PEPPERS, SPRING ONIONS, CHOPPED HERBS AND LIME JUICE ON TOP OF EACH CHICKEN PIECE.
- **SPRINKLE** WITH BLACK PEPPER, TO TASTE.
- **WRAP** THE LETTUCE LEAF AROUND.
- **PLACE** THE PARCELS IN A STEAMER.
- **STEAM** FOR 20 MINUTES.
- **SERVE** ON A WARM PLATE.

RASPBERRY SOUP

SERVES 4

250 G/9 OZ RASPBERRIES

225 ML/8 FL OZ/1 CUP DRY WHITE WINE

2 TABLESPOONS HONEY

ZEST OF 1 LIME

225 ML/8 FL OZ/1 CUP ORANGE JUICE

MINT LEAVES FOR GARNISH

- **HULL** RASPBERRIES.
- **HEAT** WINE WITH HONEY IN PAN.
- **REMOVE** FROM HEAT AND **ADD** LIME ZEST.
- **WHIZZ** WINE AND RASPBERRIES IN PROCESSOR UNTIL SMOOTH.
- **SCOOP** PURÉE INTO BOWL.
- **ADD** ORANGE JUICE.
- **COVER** AND **CHILL** FOR 4 HOURS.
- **LADLE** INTO SOUP BOWLS.
- **GARNISH** WITH MINT BEFORE SERVING.
- **PROVIDE** BEMUSED GUESTS WITH A SOUP SPOON!

To drink: an Italian white or a light red such as a French Bandol

Real sisterhood ... a bunch of dames in bathrobes throwing back M&Ms and making each other laugh.
Maxine Wilkie

There are times in your life when you need to establish an all girls' zone. For example, your relationship is at a make or break stage and you need to consult those who know you best. Call in the troops and set up a lunchtime trashing session with the gals. Don't let anyone trivialise the importance of your support group – or of a good ol' chat. And no matter how serious the problems in your relationship may seem, I guarantee that you'll end up with some belly laughs. Is there a better tonic than that? I don't think so.

Only the best is good enough for the sisterhood, so pull out all the stops.

ASPARAGUS SOUP

SERVES 4

2 MEDIUM POTATOES, PEELED

1 TABLESPOON OLIVE OIL

570 ML/1 PINT/2½ CUPS VEGETABLE STOCK

225 G/8 OZ ASPARAGUS

1 GARLIC CLOVE, CRUSHED

FRESHLY GROUND BLACK PEPPER

4 ASPARAGUS TIPS FOR GARNISH

- CHOP POTATOES.
- HEAT OLIVE OIL IN PAN.
- ADD POTATOES.
- SAUTÉ.
- ADD STOCK.
- BRING TO BOIL.
- COOK UNTIL POTATOES ARE TENDER.
- PEEL ASPARAGUS STALKS WITH POTATO PEELER.
- CUT OFF TOUGH END BITS BUT **LEAVE** TIPS.
- CHOP INTO PIECES.
- ADD ASPARAGUS AND GARLIC TO POTATOES.
- STIR UNTIL ASPARAGUS IS TENDER.
- PURÉE.

- **RETURN** SOUP TO PAN, **SEASON** WITH PEPPER, AND **REHEAT.**

- **STEAM** ASPARAGUS TIPS FOR 5 MINUTES.

- **USE** TO GARNISH SOUP.

POACHED WILD SALMON
WITH MINT HOLLANDAISE SAUCE

SERVES 4

1 TABLESPOON SEA SALT

675 G/1 ½ LB WILD SALMON (IN ONE PIECE)

- **HALF-FILL** A LARGE PAN WITH SALTED WATER.

- **BOIL** WATER.

- **PLACE** SALMON IN PAN, COVERED IN WATER.

- **SIMMER** FOR 15 MINUTES.

- **LET** FISH **SIT** IN WATER FOR 5 MORE MINUTES WITH HEAT TURNED OFF.

- **REMOVE** FROM WATER.

- **MAKE** SAUCE.

SAUCE:

140 G/5 OZ BUTTER

3 EGG YOLKS, FREE RANGE

110 ML/4 FL OZ/½ CUP WHITE WINE

1 SHALLOT, FINELY CHOPPED

JUICE OF 1 LEMON

2 TABLESPOONS FRESH MINT, CHOPPED

- **MELT** BUTTER AND **KEEP WARM.**

- **PLACE** EGG YOLKS, WINE, SHALLOTS AND LEMON JUICE IN SAUCEPAN.

- **WHISK.**

- **PUT** PAN OVER LOW HEAT.

- **CONTINUE TO WHISK** UNTIL THICK AND FOAMY.

- **DON'T OVERHEAT.**

- **REMOVE** FROM HEAT.

- **WHISK** IN MELTED BUTTER BIT BY BIT.

- **ADD** MINT.

- **SERVE** WITH SALMON.

NUTTY ICE CREAM

SERVES 4

55 G/2 OZ/½ CUP HAZELNUTS, ROASTED

100 ML/3½ FL OZ/SCANT ½ CUP HONEY

225 ML/8 FL OZ/1 CUP MILK

225 ML/8 FL OZ/1 CUP CREAM

4 EGG YOLKS, FREE RANGE

2 TABLESPOONS BRANDY

- **TOAST** HAZELNUTS UNDER GRILL.
- **HEAT** 2 TABLESPOONS HONEY IN PAN UNTIL IT STARTS TO FOAM.
- **ADD** HAZELNUTS.
- **STIR** WITH WOODEN SPOON.
- **COOL**, THEN **GRIND** HALF OF THEM IN PROCESSOR.
- **HEAT** MILK AND CREAM TO BOILING POINT IN LARGE PAN.
- **BEAT** EGG YOLKS TOGETHER WITH REMAINING HONEY.
- **WHISK** EGG MIXTURE INTO MILK AND CREAM.
- **COOK** OVER LOW HEAT.
- **STIR** CONSTANTLY FOR 10 MINUTES.
- WHEN CUSTARD MIXTURE COATS BACK OF SPOON, **TAKE** PAN OFF HEAT.
- **LET** COOL.
- **STIR** GROUND AND CHOPPED HAZELNUTS INTO CUSTARD.
- **ADD** BRANDY.
- **POUR** MIXTURE INTO FREEZER CONTAINER BIG ENOUGH TO TAKE 850 ML/1½ PINTS.
- **COVER** AND **FREEZE** UNTIL ABOUT TO SET.
- **TAKE OUT** AND **WHISK** UNTIL SMOOTH.
- **RETURN** TO CONTAINER.
- **REPLACE** IN FREEZER SECTION.
- **LEAVE** FOR A COUPLE OF HOURS UNTIL FROZEN.
- **REMOVE** FROM FREEZER 30 MINUTES BEFORE SERVING.

To drink: a nice grassy Sauvignon Blanc from New Zealand, with a Brown Brothers dessert wine to accompany the ice cream

L O N E L Y

This is a mood that has to be seized by the horns and given a firm shove in the direction of the nearest exit. Easier said than done, as this is an increasingly widespread phenomenon in today's urbanised and impersonal society. But I believe the thing holding back so many people from reaching out and coming into contact with other people is fear of rejection and feelings of low self-esteem. 'They won't want to hear from me,' and, 'Why would they be interested in me?' say those who find themselves trapped by loneliness.

The key to confronting this situation is to create an atmosphere that is genuine and relaxed, where people feel more confident about revealing their true feelings and opening up to each other. This lays the basis for forming friendships that are solid and enduring.

Why not give an afternoon tea a spin? There's something very homey about afternoon tea and conversation seems to come naturally. Not much serving, which leaves you free to chat. So get the teapot out and invite some people around for your 3 pm kick off.

First, a word on teas. Teabags are no substitute for real tea. So choose leaf tea and try some of the more exotic ones around – they can be a conversation piece if silence falls. The main tea-growing regions are Africa, India and China. Kenya and Malawi are the two big tea producers, but really I think African teas are too strong in flavour to serve for afternoon tea. China teas worth trying are: Keemun, which has a delicate smooth flavour; Lapsang Souchong, which has a distinctive smokey taste, too smokey if you ask me; Jasmine, which is usually a green tea with some jasmine leaves added, has a delicate taste – a real girlie tea; Earl Grey, a specially blended leaf scented with oil of bergamot, has a faint orangey taste.

My favourite Indian tea is Darjeeling which is grown in the foothills of the Himalayas and has a rich distinctive flavour. It's the champagne of teas.

It was in South Africa that I came across an amazing drink called Rooibosch tea. I took to it like a duck to water, so much so that back home in Ireland I'm still drinking it. It's a tea made from the plant *Aspalathus Linaris* which only grows on the slopes of the Cedar Mountains in the western region of the Cape Province. It contains no caffeine, has a low tannin content and, best of all, with a drop of milk, it's the best healthy substitute for tea going. If, like me, you can't take caffeine late at night then Rooibosch is the answer.

And then there are a hundred and one herbal teas to choose from!

SMOKED MACKEREL PATÉ

ENOUGH FOR 6

225 G/8 OZ SMOKED MACKEREL FILLETS

140 ML/5 FL OZ/½ CUP FROMAGE FRAIS

1 SMALL ONION, CHOPPED VERY FINELY

2 CLOVES GARLIC, CRUSHED

JUICE OF 1 LEMON

FRESHLY GROUND BLACK PEPPER

- **REMOVE** SKIN AND ANY BONES FROM FISH.
- **PUT** FISH IN PROCESSOR ALONG WITH ALL OTHER INGREDIENTS.
- **PROCESS** UNTIL SMOOTH.
- **PLACE** IN DISH.
- **CHILL** FOR AN HOUR.
- **SERVE** ON THIN SLICES OF WHOLEMEAL BREAD.

CUCUMBER SANDWICHES

ENOUGH FOR 6

1 CUCUMBER

8 SLICES WHOLEMEAL BREAD

4 TABLESPOONS CREAM CHEESE

FRESHLY GROUND BLACK PEPPER

- **PEEL** CUCUMBER.
- **SLICE** AS THINLY AS POSSIBLE (MOST PROCESSORS HAVE A GADGET THAT SLICES ULTRA THINLY).
- **SPREAD** CREAM CHEESE ON BREAD.
- **PLACE** CUCUMBER SLICES ON FOUR PIECES OF BREAD.
- **LAY** PIECES OF BREAD TOGETHER TO MAKE SANDWICHES.
- **CUT** CRUSTS OFF AND **CUT** SANDWICHES INTO FINGERS.
- **LAY** ON PLATE AND **SERVE** WITH WHOLEGRAIN MUSTARD ON THE SIDE.

ALMOND AND ORANGE PIE

MAKES 1 PIE

CRUST:

110 G/4 OZ/1 CUP UNBLANCHED ALMONDS

175 G/6 OZ/¾ CUP DRIED DATES, CHOPPED

3 TABLESPOONS HONEY

TOPPING:

4 ORANGES

ZEST OF 2 ORANGES

140 ML/5 FL OZ/½ CUP SOURED CREAM

140 ML/5 FL OZ/½ CUP YOGHURT

1 TABLESPOON HONEY

- **BLEND** ALMONDS IN PROCESSOR UNTIL FINE.
- **ADD** DATES.
- **BLEND** AGAIN.
- **ADD** HONEY.
- **PRESS** MIXTURE INTO A GREASED 18 CM/7 INCH FLAN DISH.
- **CHILL.**

TOPPING:

- **WHIP** SOURED CREAM AND YOGHURT IN BOWL WITH ZEST AND HONEY.
- **SPREAD** HALF OF MIXTURE ON CRUST.
- **PEEL** ORANGES AND **CUT** INTO SLICES.
- **PLACE** ORANGE SLICES ON TOP OF CREAM MIXTURE.
- **TOP** WITH MORE CREAM.
- **SERVE.**

BANANA BREAD

MAKES 1 LOAF

110 G/4 OZ/1 CUP WHOLEMEAL FLOUR

3 LEVEL TEASPOONS BAKING POWDER

PINCH OF SEA SALT

4 TABLESPOONS BUTTER

1 FREE RANGE EGG

ZEST OF 2 ORANGES

3 BANANAS, MASHED

DASH OF MILK

- **PRE-HEAT** OVEN TO 190°C/375°F/GAS MARK 5.
- **MIX** FLOUR, BAKING POWDER AND SALT.
- **RUB** IN BUTTER.
- **ADD** EGG, ORANGE ZEST AND BANANAS.
- **MIX** THOROUGHLY.
- **ADD** DROP OF MILK IF MIXTURE ISN'T STICKY.
- **PLACE** IN GREASED LOAF TIN.
- **BAKE** FOR 50 MINUTES.
- **COOL** ON RACK.

TEACAKES

MAKES 5-6

4 TABLESPOONS MILK

110 G/4 OZ/1 CUP SELF-RAISING FLOUR

2 TABLESPOONS UNSALTED BUTTER

4 TABLESPOONS CURRANTS

$\frac{1}{4}$ TEASPOON ALLSPICE

2 TABLESPOONS CANDIED PEEL

1 SMALL FREE RANGE EGG, BEATEN

JAM AND WHIPPED CREAM TO GARNISH

- **PRE-HEAT** OVEN TO 180°C/350°F/GAS MARK 4.
- **SIFT** FLOUR INTO LARGE BOWL.
- **CHOP** BUTTER INTO FLOUR, USING KNIFE.
- **STIR** CURRANTS, ALLSPICE AND PEEL INTO FLOUR.
- **MAKE** A WELL IN CENTRE.
- **STIR** IN MILK AND BEATEN EGG.
- **MIX** THOROUGHLY, MAKING SOFT DOUGH.
- **TURN** DOUGH ONTO LIGHTLY FLOURED BOARD.
- **KNEAD** UNTIL SMOOTH AND **ROLL OUT** INTO CIRCLES.
- **ARRANGE** ON LIGHTLY GREASED BAKING SHEET.
- **BAKE** FOR 20-30 MINUTES OR UNTIL CAKES ARE GOLDEN BROWN.
- **SERVE** WITH JAM AND CREAM.

SCONES

MAKES 10

225 G/8 OZ/2 CUPS PLAIN WHOLEMEAL FLOUR

2 TEASPOONS BAKING POWDER

50 G/2 OZ BUTTER

1 FREE RANGE EGG

55 G/2 OZ/SCANT $\frac{1}{2}$ CUP RAISINS

140 ML/5 FL OZ/$\frac{1}{2}$ CUP MILK

JAM AND WHIPPED CREAM TO GARNISH

- **PRE-HEAT** OVEN TO 200°C/400°F/ GAS MARK 7.
- **PUT** FLOUR AND BAKING POWDER IN BOWL.
- **CUT** BUTTER IN WITH KNIFE.
- **STIR** IN RAISINS.
- **MIX** IN MILK.
- **KNEAD** TO MAKE SOFT DOUGH.
- **TAKE** DOUGH OUT OF BOWL AND **ROLL OUT** ON FLOURED SURFACE.
- **DIVIDE** DOUGH INTO ROUND SCONES, USING COOKIE CUTTER.
- **PLACE** SCONES ON LIGHTLY GREASED BAKING TRAY.
- **BAKE** FOR 15 MINUTES OR UNTIL GOLDEN BROWN AT TOP.
- **PLACE** SCONES ON WIRE TRAY TO COOL.
- **SERVE** WHILE STILL WARM, SLICED IN HALF AND TOPPED WITH A BLOB OF WHIPPED CREAM AND JAM.

LOVING

Love is not what makes the world go round,
Love is what makes the trip worthwhile.
Franklin Jones

This is one of the most rooted and primal emotions to accompany cooking. The very act of preparing and cooking a meal with love is wonderful and it is said that food cooked with love tastes different. Many of us treasure memories of our mother preparing food and of ourselves gobbling up the results:

Helping our mothers bake.

Licking the spoon.

The smells and tastes.

The bond which can exist between mother and child is extraordinary. It can be such an unconditional love, so pure. It is not surprising that we associate the food we ate in our childhood with unconditional love. In later years, reverting back to that food brings such a comforting feeling. As the writer Amy Tan says, 'That's the way Chinese mothers show they love their children, not through hugs and kisses, but with offerings of steamed dumplings, duck's gizzard and crab.'

There's something very cosy about the food which follows: an earthy soup, a good roast chicken (with some up-to-date touches) and old-fashioned baked apples.

That, for me, is unconditional love!

CREAMY VEGETABLE SOUP

SERVES 4

2 TABLESPOONS OLIVE OIL

4 MEDIUM POTATOES, CHOPPED

2 MEDIUM CARROTS, DICED

4 STALKS CELERY, CHOPPED

3 CLOVES GARLIC, CRUSHED

1 ONION, CHOPPED

1 LARGE BROCCOLI FLORET

1.2 LITRES/2 PINTS/5 CUPS VEGETABLE STOCK

225 ML/8 FL OZ/1 CUP MILK

FRESHLY GROUND BLACK PEPPER

1 CARROT, GRATED TO GARNISH

- HEAT OLIVE OIL IN PAN.
- SAUTÉ ALL VEGETABLES IN OIL.
- POUR IN VEGETABLE STOCK.
- SIMMER FOR 20 MINUTES OR UNTIL CARROTS AND POTATOES ARE TENDER.
- PURÉE.
- REPLACE IN PAN ON LOW HEAT.
- STIR IN MILK.
- ADD PEPPER TO TASTE.
- SERVE WITH SPRINKLING OF GRATED CARROT.

LEMON ROASTED CHICKEN

SERVES 4

3 LEMONS, SLICED

1.8 KG/4 LB FREE RANGE CHICKEN

3 TABLESPOONS BUTTER

FRESHLY GROUND BLACK PEPPER

20 CLOVES GARLIC, UNPEELED

LETTUCE LEAVES TO GARNISH

DASH OF BALSAMIC VINEGAR

- **PRE-HEAT** OVEN TO 220°C/425°F/GAS MARK 7.
- **PLACE** SLICED LEMONS INTO CAVITY OF CHICKEN.
- **SMEAR** OUTSIDE OF CHICKEN WITH BUTTER AND A LITTLE PEPPER.
- **PLACE** CHICKEN IN ROASTING TIN IN OVEN.
- **BASTE** AFTER 20 MINUTES.
- **TURN** OVEN DOWN TO 190°C/375°F/GAS MARK 5.
- **PLACE** GARLIC IN TIN ALONGSIDE CHICKEN.
- **COOK** FOR APPROXIMATELY 50 MINUTES MORE.
- **TEST** WITH SKEWER IN CHICKEN THIGH – IF JUICES RUN CLEAR THEN CHICKEN IS COOKED.
- **LET** CHICKEN **REST** OUT OF OVEN FOR 10-15 MINUTES BEFORE SERVING.
- **SERVE** EACH CHICKEN PORTION WITH 5 CLOVES OF ROASTED GARLIC.
- **SPRINKLE** LETTUCE WITH OLIVE OIL AND A DASH OF BALSAMIC VINEGAR.
- **SERVE** WITH STIR-FRY BRUSSEL SPROUTS.

STIR-FRY BRUSSEL SPROUTS

SERVES 4

20 BRUSSEL SPROUTS

1 TABLESPOON OLIVE OIL

FRESHLY GROUND BLACK PEPPER

- **PEEL** FIRST LAYER OFF SPROUTS.
- **CUT** SPROUTS FINELY INTO THIN STRIPS.

- **HEAT** OIL IN A WOK.
- **TOSS** BRUSSEL SPROUTS INTO WOK.
- **STIR** QUICKLY FOR ABOUT 2 MINUTES OR UNTIL SPROUTS START TO BROWN AT EDGES.
- **SPRINKLE** WITH PEPPER.
- **SERVE**.

MUM'S BAKED APPLES

SERVES 4

4 COOKING APPLES, 1 PER PERSON

$\frac{1}{2}$ TEASPOON GROUND CINNAMON

$\frac{1}{4}$ TEASPOON GROUND CLOVES

4 TABLESPOONS RAISINS, CHOPPED

4 TABLESPOONS MAPLE SYRUP

ZEST OF 1 ORANGE

ZEST OF 1 LEMON

2 TABLESPOONS BUTTER

CRÈME FRAÎCHE

- **PRE-HEAT** OVEN TO 190°C/375°F/GAS MARK 5.
- **CORE** APPLES.
- **MIX** ALL REMAINING INGREDIENTS EXCEPT CRÈME FRAÎCHE IN BOWL.
- **STUFF** APPLES WITH MIXTURE.
- **PLACE** IN OVENPROOF DISH.
- **BAKE** FOR 40-45 MINUTES.
- **SERVE** WITH SPOONFULS OF CRÈME FRAÎCHE.

To drink: a white Alsace wine

M I S C H I E V O U S

Happiness is having a large, loving, caring, closeknit family ...
in another city.
George Burns

The relatives are coming! This is a call to action.

The only way to deal with the emotional minefield of a visit from your relatives or in-laws is to be naughty – but nice. Think of the visit as an opportunity to make it clear that you do not want them to come over again. This is no time for subtlety, I favour the pneumatic drill approach – make a devastating impact.

'But they're my relatives!!' I hear you say. This is no time for pathetic protests, just remind yourself of all the bile that they have served up in your direction over the years and set yourself on course to deliver the mother of all revenge dinners. If it makes you feel any better, remember that the old saying, 'Blood is thicker than water', is a sinister phrase repeated by people with little sense and no experience of real life.

Not convinced yet? Then skip this chapter because quite frankly you're only wasting your time. But for those of you who, like me, are determined to cook up a meal that your in-laws will never forget, let's get down to business. You've got to dish up a meal which they'll eat but which will guarantee a return visit is permanently off the menu. This will require deploying high levels of nerve. Now, *I* draw the line at poisoning, but don't let me cramp *your* style!

First, a little classic. Guaranteed exotic, these eggs look just like the Oriental speciality which was to bury eggs in pots underground for a millennium and then eat them as a supreme delicacy.

ORIENTAL QUAIL'S EGGS

2 QUAIL'S EGGS PER PERSON

3 TABLESPOONS STRONGLY BREWED BLACK COFFEE

3 TABLESPOONS OLIVE OIL

- ■ HARD-BOIL EGGS IN BOILING WATER.

- ■ REMOVE EGGS AND LET COOL.

- ■ TAP EGGS LIGHTLY ON HARD SURFACE TO PRODUCE TINY CRACKS ON SHELLS.

- ■ MIX COFFEE WITH OLIVE OIL AND POUR INTO SMALL BOWL.

- ■ IMMERSE EGGS IN LIQUID AND LEAVE SUBMERGED FOR 8 HOURS.

- **DRAIN, SHELL** AND **CUT** EGGS IN HALF.

- **SURPRISE!** THE WHITES NOW HAVE A MARBLED EFFECT AND THE YOLKS LOOK DISGUSTING AS WELL

- **ARRANGE** THESE ENTICING TITBITS ON BED OF LETTUCE AND **SERVE.**

Naturally, you can claim you buried your eggs in a hole in the back garden a year ago, and can marvel at how the worms didn't get at them.

The main course is a real humdinger. Simple yet filling, it's called the Kitchen Sink Tomato Sandwich. It comes from *White Trash Cooking*, the highly-rated American cookbook by Ernest Matthew Mickler, and, as the name implies, this cooking is for a special kind of folk. Your relatives must fall into this category.

The following ingredients are enough to make one sandwich. Believe me, it will be enough.

KITCHEN SINK TOMATO SANDWICH

FOR EACH SANDWICH
1 LARGE RIPE TOMATO
1 LARGE DOLLOP MAYONNAISE
2 SLICES WHITE BREAD
FRESHLY GROUND BLACK PEPPER
PINCH OF SEA SALT

- **SLICE** TOMATOES INTO LARGE THICK SLICES.

- **SPREAD** MAYO GENEROUSLY ON BOTH SLICES OF BREAD.

- **ARRANGE** TOMATOES ON BED OF MAYO.

- **SPRINKLE** WITH PEPPER AND SALT.

- THE NEXT BIT IS TRICKY. **ENCOURAGE** YOUR GUESTS TO GATHER AROUND THE KITCHEN SINK.

- **ASK** THEM TO ROLL UP THEIR SLEEVES SO THAT WHEN THEY MUNCH ON THE SANDWICH THE JUICE WILL RUN DOWN THEIR ELBOWS AND INTO THE KITCHEN SINK.

If they haven't been thoroughly wowed by this stage, please don't worry, the best is yet to come. What appears to be a perfectly acceptable and delicious dessert quickly reveals itself to be something else completely ...

PARSNIP PIE SURPRISE

MAKES 1 PIE

PASTRY:

175 G/6 OZ/1 CUP PLAIN FLOUR

85 G/3 OZ CHILLED BUTTER, IN CUBES

2 TABLESPOONS COLD WATER

25 CM/10 INCH LOOSE-BOTTOMED FLUTED FLAN TIN

PIE FILLING:

4 PARSNIPS

4 TABLESPOONS MAPLE SYRUP

PINCH MIXED SPICES

ZEST AND JUICE OF 1 LIME

2 EGG YOLKS, FREE RANGE

100 ML/3$\frac{1}{2}$ FL OZ/SCANT $\frac{1}{2}$ CUP CRÈME FRAÎCHE

100 ML/3$\frac{1}{2}$ FL OZ/SCANT $\frac{1}{2}$ CUP CREAM

ZEST OF 1 ORANGE

- **PRE-HEAT** OVEN TO 200°C/400°F/GAS MARK 6.
- **SIEVE** FLOUR INTO LARGE BOWL.
- **ADD** BUTTER.
- **RUB** IN WITH FINGERTIPS UNTIL MIXTURE RESEMBLES FINE BREADCRUMBS.
- **MIX** IN ENOUGH WATER TO MAKE A SOFT PLIABLE DOUGH.
- **WRAP** DOUGH IN CLINGFILM AND **LEAVE** IN FRIDGE TO CHILL FOR ABOUT 30 MINUTES.
- **ROLL** DOUGH ON A FLOURED SURFACE AND **LINE** FLAN TIN.
- **CHOP** PARSNIPS INTO CUBES.
- **COOK, DRAIN** AND **MASH.**
- **MIX** PURÉE WITH SYRUP, MIXED SPICES, ZEST, JUICE OF LIME AND EGG YOLKS.
- **BEAT** UNTIL SMOOTH.
- **TAKE** DOUGH FROM FRIDGE AND **ROLL OUT** ON LIGHTLY FLOURED SURFACE.
- **LINE** FLAN TIN.
- **POUR** PURÉE INTO PASTRY CASE IN FLAN TIN.
- **BAKE** FOR 10 MINUTES.
- **REDUCE** TEMPERATURE TO 180°C/350°F/GAS MARK 4.

- **CONTINUE BAKING** FOR ANOTHER 30 MINUTES.
- **MIX** CRÈME FRAÎCHE AND CREAM FOR TOPPING.
- **SPREAD** ON PIE.
- **DECORATE** WITH ZEST OF ORANGE.
- **SERVE** HOT.

And the surprise? Well, that this pie, masquerading as banana, is actually made from a root vegetable.

You can be assured that your relatives will not want a repeat performance of a meal like this. It's not that the food wasn't nice, it's just that they won't ever trust you again. They might even take pity on you and buy you Delia Smith's latest tome. One thing is for sure though, they will never ever return for another meal. Mission accomplished.

To drink: the rellys are sure to appreciate sweet and cheap German white wine

Nostalgia ain't what it used to be.
Graffito

Yearning for the past is not a thing to be encouraged on a regular basis. It's far healthier to live in the present. But a bit of nostalgia now and then is no bad thing. Usually it's the happiest period of our lives we reminisce about mistily – childhood becomes one long summer holiday, or adolescence becomes one long party. Isn't memory a funny thing? It edits out the bad bits so that usually the past becomes pleasing. This is what gives nostalgia its charm.

I hold a glamourised version of the sixties in my head even though, being born in 1961, I missed out on the real action of that decade. I once met someone who talked knowledgeably about Woodstock, but then I worked out that he would have been only three years old at the time – talk about imagination!

Music is one great inspirer of nostalgia, sense of smell is another, but food is equally powerful – nothing evokes childhood like the foods we imagine we ate during that time. I have concocted a menu here which I describe as 'nostalgia on a plate'.

OIRISH STEW

SERVES 6

1 TABLESPOON OLIVE OIL

6 MUTTON CHOPS

6 POTATOES

6 ONIONS

6 CARROTS

570 ML/1 PINT/2½ CUPS VEGETABLE STOCK

FRESHLY GROUND BLACK PEPPER

1 TABLESPOON CHOPPED PARSLEY

225 ML/8 FL OZ/1 CUP CREAM, OPTIONAL, BUT LUXURIOUS

- **PRE-HEAT** OVEN TO 180°C/350°F/GAS MARK 4.

- **HEAT** OIL IN PAN.

- **BROWN** AND **SEAL** CHOPS.

- **PEEL** AND **CUT** POTATOES, ONIONS AND CARROTS INTO LARGE BITE-SIZED PIECES.

- **ADD** VEGETABLES TO PAN.

- **STIR** IN VEGETABLE STOCK.
- **ADD** PEPPER.
- **TRANSFER** CONTENTS OF PAN TO COVERED CASSEROLE DISH.
- **PLACE** IN OVEN FOR APPROXIMATELY 1 HOUR.
- **TAKE OUT** OF OVEN.
- **STIR** IN CREAM.
- **BEFORE** SERVING **ADD** PARSLEY.

COLCANNON

SERVES 6

450 G/1 LB POTATOES, PEELED
2 ONIONS, FINELY CHOPPED
$\frac{1}{2}$ GREEN CABBAGE, FINELY CHOPPED
4 TABLESPOONS BUTTER
FRESHLY GROUND BLACK PEPPER

- **STEAM** POTATOES, ONIONS AND CABBAGE.
- **MASH** ALL VEGETABLES TOGETHER.
- **ADD** BUTTER AND PEPPER.
- **SERVE.**

BACK TO ROOTS VEG

SERVES 6

450 G/1 LB TURNIPS
1 LARGE ONION, CHOPPED
1 TABLESPOON OLIVE OIL
FRESHLY GROUND BLACK PEPPER

- **PEEL** AND **CUBE** TURNIP.
- **STEAM** TURNIP FOR ABOUT 20 MINUTES.
- **SAUTÉ** ONION IN OLIVE OIL UNTIL BROWN ON EDGES.
- **MASH** TURNIP TO PURÉE.
- **ADD** ONION TO TURNIP.
- **SPRINKLE** WITH PEPPER.

I prefer to make this in individual ramekin dishes:

BREAD AND BUTTER PUD

SERVES 6

4 TABLESPOONS BUTTER

6 SLICES OF 2-DAY OLD WHOLEMEAL BREAD, CRUSTS REMOVED

3 TABLESPOONS DRIED DATES, FINELY CHOPPED

3 TABLESPOONS RAISINS

$\frac{1}{4}$ TEASPOON CINNAMON

$\frac{1}{4}$ TEASPOON NUTMEG

ZEST OF 1 ORANGE

225 ML/8 FL OZ/1 CUP MILK

1 FREE RANGE EGG

3 TABLESPOONS MAPLE SYRUP

CREAM TO SERVE

(10 CM/4 INCH RAMEKIN DISHES)

- **PRE-HEAT** OVEN TO 180°C/350°F/GAS MARK 4.
- **BUTTER** 6 SLICES OF BREAD ON ONE SIDE.
- LIGHTLY **BUTTER** RAMEKIN DISHES.
- **MIX** DATES, RAISINS, NUTMEG, CINNAMON AND ZEST OF ORANGE.
- **PLACE** ENOUGH BREAD IN EACH DISH TO COVER BASE.
- **SPRINKLE** WITH HALF THE DRIED FRUIT.
- **PUT** ANOTHER LAYER OF BREAD ON TOP IN EACH RAMEKIN, AND **SPRINKLE** REMAINDER OF FRUIT OVER THIS.
- **BEAT** MILK AND EGG TOGETHER WITH MAPLE SYRUP.
- **DIVIDE** THIS MIXTURE EVENLY BETWEEN RAMEKINS.
- **LEAVE** FOR 15 MINUTES SO LIQUID IS ABSORBED BY BREAD.
- **PLACE** IN OVEN FOR ABOUT 20 MINUTES OR UNTIL GOLDEN BROWN ON TOP.
- **SERVE** WITH DOLLOP OF CREAM.

To drink: a chilled Guinness

OPTIMISTIC

It does not matter how small you are if you have faith and a plan of action.
Fidel Castro

This is one of my very favourite moods. Optimism is all about hope, new beginnings and the anticipation of a happy outcome to whatever situation you find yourself in. And the essence of optimism in Ireland must be to plan an *al fresco* meal!

Time to pack up and picnic! Head for the coast, the mountains or a lake, and take a chance on the weather.

There are a few essentials necessary to a good picnic:

- Four people willing to go for it, for whom eating off the bonnet of a car is as satisfying as dining at a linen-covered table lit by candles
- Fresh crusty bread, preferably straight from the oven of a specialist baker
- A few bottles of really good wine
- Real wine glasses, none of your paper cups, thank you very much
- Food that tastes as good as if you were eating indoors

Here are some tasty dishes to create a memorable moveable feast:

OUTDOORS OMELETTE

SERVES 6

900 G/2 LB PEELED POTATOES

SEA SALT

FRESHLY GROUND BLACK PEPPER

110 ML/4 FL OZ/½ CUP OLIVE OIL

2 LARGE ONIONS, PEELED AND CHOPPED

6 FREE RANGE EGGS

- **SLICE** POTATOES THINLY.
- **SEASON** WITH PINCH OF SALT AND PEPPER.
- **HEAT** ¼ CUP OF OIL IN PAN.
- **FRY** POTATOES UNTIL GOLDEN BROWN.
- **SAUTÉ** ONIONS IN ANOTHER PAN.
- **BEAT** EGGS IN BOWL.
- **ADD** ONIONS AND PINCH OF SALT.
- **DRAIN** POTATOES.
- **STIR** INTO EGG MIX.
- **HEAT UP** REMAINDER OF OIL IN NON-STICK PAN.
- **TURN** WHOLE MIXTURE INTO PAN.
- **COOK** OVER MEDIUM HEAT UNTIL TOP IS FIRM.
- **PLACE** LARGE DINNERPLATE OVER PAN, MAKING SURE IT IS BIGGER THAN PAN.
- **TURN** WHOLE LOT UPSIDE-DOWN, SO THAT OMELETTE PLOPS OUT ONTO PLATE.
- **CUT** INTO SLICES WHEN COOLED.
- **PUT** INTO BOX TO TRANSPORT.

BLUE SKIES PEPPERS

SERVES 6

6 PEPPERS – GREEN, RED, YELLOW, ORANGE ONES

4 TABLESPOONS OLIVE OIL

SELECTION OF SALAD LEAVES

- **PRE-HEAT** OVEN TO 200°C/400°F/GAS MARK 6.
- **ROAST** PEPPERS IN OVEN FOR 30 MINUTES.
- **CHECK** AND **TURN** EVERY 10 MINUTES.

- **REMOVE** WHEN BROWN.
- **PLACE** IN POLYTHENE BAG FOR 30 MINUTES.
- **REMOVE** AND **PEEL**.
- **REMOVE** STALKS AND SEEDS.
- **CUT** FLESH INTO THIN STRIPS.
- **PUT** INTO CONTAINER TO TRANSPORT.
- **WASH** AND **DRY** LETTUCE LEAVES.
- **PLACE** IN SEPARATE CONTAINER FOR TRANSPORT.

PICNIC PRAWNS

SERVES 6

24 PRAWNS, 4 PER PERSON

- **STEAM** PRAWNS IN SHELLS UNTIL PINK.
- **ALLOW TO COOL** AND **PEEL OFF** SHELLS.
- **PLACE** IN CONTAINER FOR PICNIC.
- **MAKE UP** HAZELNUT DRESSING AS ACCOMPANIMENT.

HAZELNUT DRESSING

1 TEASPOON HAZELNUTS, FINELY CHOPPED
6 TABLESPOONS OLIVE OIL
1 TABLESPOON LEMON JUICE
1 TABLESPOON DIJON MUSTARD
1 TEASPOON HONEY
FRESHLY GROUND BLACK PEPPER

- **GRILL** HAZELNUTS UNTIL BEGINNING TO BROWN.
- **PLACE** ALL INGREDIENTS INTO JAM-JAR AND **SHAKE**.
- **SERVE** FROM JAM-JAR.

CHEESE AL FRESCO

Take a selection of Irish farmhouse cheeses, fresh fruit and wholemeal biscuits to end the picnic with panache

To drink: a spicy white from Alsace, perhaps a Gewurztraminer

Looked at in the right light any food might be thought an aphrodisiac.
Diana Ackerman

Most people associate this emotion with love and lust (though I know lots of people who seem more passionate about sport or music than about sex).

But I think that if true passion exists between two people you are wasting your time interfering with this forcefield of sexual energy that blinds a couple to the world around them. You might as well serve up stale toast and cold tea as go to the trouble of preparing an elaborate meal.

The morning after, on the other hand, has a curiously sobering effect on even the most romantic and moonstruck of lovers. Bleary eyes, tossed hair and an urge to visit the bathroom can all have a very passion-quenching effect.

Don't worry, passion is also a great appetiser, so breakfast needs to go beyond cereal and a mug of coffee. Try this light, lovely and luscious breakfast in bed.

FROTHY FRUIT JUICE

SERVES 2, OF COURSE

2 ORANGES

4 PINK GRAPEFRUIT

CRUSHED ICE

- **JUICE** ORANGES AND PINK GRAPEFRUIT.
- **POUR** INTO JUG OVER ICE.

Follow with freshly brewed coffee.

ORANGE PANCAKES

MAKES 4

225 G/8 OZ/1 CUP PLAIN FLOUR

PINCH OF SEA SALT

1 SMALL FREE RANGE EGG, BEATEN

140 ML/5 FL OZ /²⁄₃ CUP ORANGE JUICE

1 TEASPOON OLIVE OIL

ORANGE SEGMENTS

CRÈME FRAÎCHE

ZEST OF 1 ORANGE

MAPLE SYRUP

- **COMBINE** FLOUR AND SALT.
- **STIR** IN EGG.
- **BEAT** IN ORANGE JUICE.
- **ADD** OIL.
- **LEAVE** STANDING FOR 30 MINUTES.
- **HEAT** PAN WITH DROP OF OIL.
- **POUR** LADLE OF BATTER ONTO PAN.
- **SPREAD OUT** IN CIRCLE.
- **FLIP** PANCAKE OVER AFTER 1 MINUTE.
- **COOK** FOR ANOTHER MINUTE.
- **SERVE** WITH SEGMENT OF ORANGE AND SCOOP OF CRÈME FRAÎCHE, TOPPED WITH ORANGE ZEST AND SWIRL OF MAPLE SYRUP.

Passionfruit Yoghurt

Serves 2

2 passionfruit

250 ml/9 fl oz/scant 1 ¼ cups natural yoghurt

Honey to taste

- **Scoop out** flesh of passionfruit.
- **Keep** juice.
- **Add** flesh and juice to yoghurt.
- **Stir** together.
- **Add** honey to taste.
- **Serve** in stemmed glasses.

Succulent Salmon

Serves 2

2 slices wild smoked salmon

3 free range eggs

Freshly ground black pepper

1 tablespoon milk

1 teaspoon butter

2 wholegrain muffins, split and toasted

Wedges of lemon

2 teaspoons chopped chives

- **Line** 2 ramekin dishes with pieces of smoked salmon.
- **Whisk** eggs in bowl with some pepper and dash of milk.
- **Melt** butter in pan.
- **Pour** eggs into pan.
- **Keep** stirring until eggs are scrambled.
- **Place** in salmon-lined ramekin dishes.
- **Fold** salmon over top.
- **Turn** bundles out on halved muffin.
- **Serve** with wedge of lemon.
- **Sprinkle** with chives.

Let your food be your medicine; let your medicine be your food.
Hippocrates

Your stomach is in a knot, your mind is in a muddle, you feel queasy. You've got some bad news or someone has been downright nasty to your face. You might not feel like food at all but a careful choice together with the act of eating can provide a sense of comfort and may stabilise your stomach.

There's no doubt about it, food can change how you feel. It can help.

First of all make yourself a cup of peppermint tea – either from a tea bag or from a handful of crushed fresh mint with hot water (SEE 'Calm'). Mint soothes nauseous stomachs.

When your insides feel more settled, go back to basics and eat plain and simple food.

GRILLED FISH

SERVES 2

2 PORTIONS WHITE FISH – COD OR MONKFISH

2 TABLESPOONS OLIVE OIL

PINCH OF SEA SALT

FRESHLY GROUND BLACK PEPPER

- **BRUSH** FISH WITH SOME OLIVE OIL.
- **POUR** MORE OIL ON FOIL-LINED GRILL.
- **HEAT** TO A VERY HIGH TEMPERATURE.
- **GRILL** FOR 4 MINUTES ON EACH SIDE OR UNTIL FISH IS COOKED THROUGH – THIS WILL DEPEND ON THICKNESS.
- **SERVE** WITH GRILLED VEGETABLES.

GRILLED VEGETABLES

SERVES 2

1 RED ONION

1 RED PEPPER

1 YELLOW PEPPER

1 COURGETTE

6 BUTTON MUSHROOMS, 3 PER PERSON

OLIVE OIL

DASH OF BALSAMIC VINEGAR

- **WASH** VEGETABLES AND **DE-SEED** PEPPERS.
- **CUT** INTO LARGE CHUNKS.
- **BRUSH** WITH OLIVE OIL.
- **PLACE** UNDER HOT GRILL.
- **COOK** FOR 6 MINUTES.
- **PLACE** FISH AND MIXTURE OF VEGETABLES ON PLATE.
- **SPRINKLE** WITH BALSAMIC VINEGAR.

FRUIT KEBABS 'N' CREAM

SERVES 2

12-INCH WOODEN SKEWERS

YOUR CHOICE OF FRUIT

110 ML/4 FL OZ/$\frac{1}{2}$ CUP MAPLE SYRUP

- **PLACE** PIECES OF FRUIT, EG BANANA, KIWI, PEAR, SOME GRAPES, STRAWBERRIES ON SKEWER.
- **PUT** FRUIT-LADEN SKEWER IN DISH.
- **MARINATE** IN MAPLE SYRUP FOR 20 MINUTES.
- **PLACE** SKEWERS ON FOIL-LINED GRILL PAN, UNDER HOT GRILL, TURNING WHEN FRUIT BROWNS.

FOR CREAM:

225 G/8 OZ/1 CUP CASHEW NUTS, UNSALTED

55 ML/2 FL OZ/$\frac{1}{4}$ CUP WATER

- **BLEND** NUTS AND WATER IN PROCESSOR UNTIL LIQUID.
- TO THIN, JUST **ADD** MORE WATER.
- **SERVE** FRUIT KEBABS WITH CASHEW NUT CREAM ON SIDE.

To drink: a Chardonnay from Chile

RAGING

Great fury, like great whisky, requires long fermentation.
Truman Capote

The first time I visited a professional kitchen I was struck by the solidity and permanence of the pots, pans and general tools of the trade in the kitchen. I had imagined all sorts of delicate stainless-steel saucepans and rapier-thin knives which would delicately slice and chop all manner of foods. Instead I saw heavy black iron and steel pots, knives like medieval war weapons and chopping boards made from great flat slabs of wood, worn and scarred from constant use.

I asked the chef the reason for this and, almost under his breath, he muttered, 'Have you ever seen mood swings in a kitchen?'

It all made sense in an instant.

Then I got to thinking. This equipment is made to outlast some furious abuse. There's no better place to find yourself in a rage than in a kitchen.

So let go of some of that long-fermented rage by letting off steam.

Eat with a long-suffering friend whom you have instructed to agree with everything you say, compliment you wherever possible, and smile benignly if you suddenly scream or bang something off the table.

ALL STEAMED-UP SEAFOOD

SERVES 2

6 PRAWNS

12 CLAMS

12 MUSSELS

10-12 MUSHROOMS, SLICED

5 SPRING ONIONS, CHOPPED

3 TABLESPOONS SOY SAUCE

2 CLOVES GARLIC, CHOPPED

SESAME SEEDS TO GARNISH

- **STEAM** CLAMS AND MUSSELS IN BAMBOO STEAMER OVER POT OF BOILING WATER.
- **ADD** PRAWNS AFTER 1 MINUTE.
- **COOK** UNTIL PRAWNS ARE PINK AND CURLED — ABOUT 2 MINUTES.
- **STEAM** MUSHROOMS AND SPRING ONIONS FOR ABOUT 3 MINUTES.
- **WARM** SOY SAUCE IN A PAN.
- **ADD** GARLIC.
- **SIMMER** FOR 3 MINUTES.
- **ADD** STEAMED SHELLFISH.
- **COAT** INGREDIENTS WITH SOY SAUCE.
- **SERVE** SEAFOOD IN PAN OVER BED OF MUSHROOMS AND ONIONS.
- **SPRINKLE** WITH SESAME SEEDS.

RIOT RAISIN' PUDDING

SERVES 2

3 TABLESPOONS BUTTER

3 TABLESPOONS RAISINS

4 TABLESPOONS MAPLE SYRUP

ZEST OF 1 LEMON

1 FREE RANGE EGG, BEATEN

25 G/1 OZ WALNUTS, CHOPPED

85 G/3 OZ/GENEROUS $\frac{1}{2}$ CUP SELF RAISING FLOUR

1 TEASPOON BAKING POWDER

1 TABLESPOON MILK

DOLLOP OF CRÈME FRAÎCHE

- GREASE 570 ML/1 PINT PUDDING BOWL.
- BEAT BUTTER AND SYRUP TOGETHER.
- ADD LEMON ZEST.
- ADD BEATEN EGG.
- MIX IN RAISINS.
- ADD WALNUTS.
- STIR IN SIEVED FLOUR AND BAKING POWDER.
- MIX TO THICK BATTER.
- ADD ENOUGH MILK TO GIVE DROPPING CONSISTENCY.
- POUR INTO BOWL.
- COVER BOWL WITH DOUBLED GREASEPROOF PAPER.
- SECURE WITH STRING.
- PUT BOWL INTO PAN OF BOILING WATER.
- STEAM FOR APPROXIMATELY 2 HOURS, TOPPING UP OCCASIONALLY WITH WATER.
- TURN PUDDING OUT.
- SERVE WITH CREAM OR CRÈME FRAÎCHE.

To drink: for the steamed shellfish, an Australian Sauvignon Blanc; for the pudding a dessert wine.

Within our darkest moments, our brightest treasures can be found.
Marcus Allen

Feeling under the weather? Maybe it's dark, cold and drizzly. Maybe you're just feeling blue. Honey, grab that apron, and get busy in the kitchen! You need a sunshine meal.

Never underestimate the effects of colour – especially in cooking. You could create a red meal, or a yellow one, but orange is my favourite gloom-buster.

This is also a great theme for a cheer-yourself-up dinner party.

First, prioritise:

Juice yourself some fresh orange juice, this is crucial because it's going to be the base for your drink while you prepare your meal. This will definitely perk you up; if it doesn't, you may be beyond help.

─── ORANGE VODKA ───

SERVES 1

- **POUR** A GLASS OF CHILLED ORANGE JUICE.
- **ADD** IRRESPONSIBLE AMOUNTS OF VODKA.
- **SIP** AS YOU COOK.

Next, food.

CHEERFUL CARROT SOUP

SERVES 4

1 TABLESPOON OLIVE OIL

1 ONION, CHOPPED

450 G/1 LB CARROTS, PEELED AND CHOPPED

570 ML/1 PINT /2½ CUPS VEGETABLE STOCK

ZEST OF ½ ORANGE

140 ML/5 FL OZ/SCANT ⅔ CUP ORANGE JUICE

FRESHLY GROUND BLACK PEPPER

CREAM TO SERVE

- **HEAT** OIL IN PAN.
- **ADD** ONION.
- **SAUTÉ** UNTIL TRANSLUCENT BUT NOT BROWN.
- **ADD** CARROTS.
- **COOK** FOR 10 MINUTES, STIRRING.
- **ADD** STOCK.
- **SIMMER** FOR 30 MINUTES.
- **WHIZZ** IN PROCESSOR.
- **RETURN** TO PAN.
- **ADD** ORANGE ZEST, ORANGE JUICE AND PEPPER .
- **HEAT** THROUGH.
- **SERVE** WITH A SWIRL OF CREAM ON TOP.

SUNNY PEPPERS

SERVES 4

4 ORANGE PEPPERS

225 G/8 OZ MINCED LAMB

OLIVE OIL

1 LARGE ONION, FINELY CHOPPED

2 MEDIUM TOMATOES, PEELED AND CHOPPED

4 SPRING ONIONS, CHOPPED

300 G/11 OZ/2 CUPS COOKED SHORT GRAIN RICE

3 TABLESPOONS PINE KERNELS

- **PRE-HEAT** OVEN TO 190°C/375°F/GAS MARK 5.
- **CUT OFF** STEM END OF EACH PEPPER AND **SET ASIDE**.
- **REMOVE** CORE AND SEEDS.
- **BROWN** LAMB WITH A LITTLE OLIVE OIL.
- **ADD** CHOPPED ONION AND **SOFTEN**.
- **ADD** IN TOMATOES AND SPRING ONIONS, AND **COOK** FOR A FEW MINUTES.
- **STIR** IN COOKED RICE AND PINE KERNELS.
- **PLACE** PEPPERS IN ROASTING TIN.
- **PACK** FILLING INTO INDIVIDUAL PEPPERS.
- **COVER** WITH TOPS.
- **BRUSH** OLIVE OIL OVER PEPPERS.
- **BAKE** FOR 30 MINUTES OR UNTIL PEPPERS ARE BROWN IN PLACES.

MANGO SORBET

SERVES 4

2 LARGE RIPE MANGOES

110 ML/4 FL OZ/½ CUP ORANGE JUICE

FRESH MINT TO GARNISH

- **PURÉE** MANGOS AND ORANGE JUICE IN PROCESSOR.
- **POUR** INTO CONTAINER.
- **FREEZE** FOR ABOUT TWO HOURS UNTIL MUSHY.
- **BLEND** THIS MIXTURE.
- **RE-FREEZE** UNTIL FIRM.
- **SERVE** WITH SPRIG OF MINT.

Here are some seriously delicious orange-looking cocktails. Serve during the meal and after. The measurements are for one large glass – increase quantities as you like.

BLAST FROM THE PAST

2 TABLESPOONS TEQUILA

1 TABLESPOON GALLIANO

1 TABLESPOON VODKA

4 TABLESPOONS PEACH JUICE

- **MIX** INGREDIENTS WELL AND **SERVE** OVER CRUSHED ICE.

SUNBURST

2 TABLESPOONS WHISKY

1 TABLESPOON TRIPLE SEC OR COINTREAU

4 TABLESPOONS MANGO JUICE

- **MIX** INGREDIENTS WELL AND **SERVE** OVER CRUSHED ICE.

SUNSTROKE

4 TABLESPOONS BRANDY

4 TABLESPOONS APRICOT JUICE

2 TABLESPOONS ORANGE JUICE

- **MIX** INGREDIENTS WELL AND **SERVE** OVER CRUSHED ICE.

STRESSED

When I am all hassled about something, I always stop and ask myself what difference it will make in the evolution of the human species in the next ten million years and that question always helps me to get back my perspective.
Anne Wilson Schaef

Ten parking fines on your kitchen table?

Two gas bills to pay and the next one due in seven days?

The exhaust pipe has fallen off your car and the dentist advises you that your child's expensive brace has to be done this year?

And this is just for starters.

Your boss tells you of impending changes in work practices that mean higher productivity requirements, less hours to do it in and greater job insecurity.

The government is promising higher taxes, increases in interest rates and the chance of higher education bills.

What do you do?

Go fishing ?

Drop out?

Lock yourself into the airing cupboard?

Stress is part of everyone's life, it has a plus side – it gets you motivated to do things. But these days, it is easy for stress levels to get out of hand. The question is, how much stress is too much?

If you feel that there's too much going on, that you're out of control and surrounded by chaos, if your sleep patterns are disturbed, and you are irritable for no reason, you may be suffering from too much stress. You need to downshift. Yes, this means cut the crap out of your life. Take a long hard look at your lifestyle – and then just drop what you don't need. Simplify. Diet can help. Drop coffee, tea, white sugar and alcohol. They all interfere with the body's ability to cope with stress. Substitute herb teas, honey and interesting fruit juice cocktails. The best foods of all for dealing with stress are uncooked vegetables and fruit. As health guru Leslie Kenton says in *Raw Energy*, 'raw food keeps the acid-alkaline balance in the body, this helps you to feel calm and collected and better equipped to deal with stress.' The simpler the food – the less fancy sauces and processed foods you eat – the easier it is for your digestion to do its work, and the greater your body's vitamin and mineral intake.

A glass of freshly squeezed juice in the morning is a great start. Try to include a side or main salad in the rest of the day's eating and you're well on the way to giving your body what it really needs to help in the daily battle against hassle.

And most important of all, keep away from the booze.

CELERY JUICE

SERVES 1

5 STALKS CELERY

ICE CUBES

- JUICE CELERY STALKS.
- POP A FEW ICE CUBES INTO A GLASS.
- POUR JUICE OVER ICE.
- SIP.

Simple Salad

SERVES 1

1 RED ONION

$\frac{1}{2}$ CUCUMBER

$\frac{1}{2}$ HEAD OF ICEBERG LETTUCE

2 TABLESPOONS SUNFLOWER SEEDS

1 AVOCADO

- **CHOP** ONION AND CUCUMBER VERY FINELY.
- **PUT** WASHED LETTUCE LEAVES IN BOWL.
- **ADD** SUNFLOWER SEEDS, ONION AND CUCUMBER.
- **CUT** AVOCADO INTO CUBES AND **ARRANGE** ON TOP OF SALAD.

DRESSING:

3 TABLESPOONS OLIVE OIL

JUICE OF 1 LEMON

1 TEASPOON MUSTARD SEED

FRESHLY GROUND BLACK PEPPER

- **MIX** ALL INGREDIENTS TOGETHER WELL.
- **DRIZZLE** OVER SALAD.

Tutti-Fruitti

SERVES 1

TAKE 5 DIFFERENT TYPES OF FRUIT — APPLE, PEAR, ORANGE, BANANA AND PLUM

- **PEEL** AND **CHOP** FRUIT, EXCEPT FOR PLUM.
- **JUICE** PLUM.
- **POUR** PLUM JUICE OVER CHOPPED-UP FRUIT.
- **PLACE** IN FREEZER FOR 10 MINUTES.
- **SERVE** WITH YOGHURT.

Munching a sandwich as you hurtle earthwards at 130 miles per hour might be considered a thrill by some folks. Not in my book, though, it's not.

What about adventurous eating? Would you eat from a market stall in Jaipur?

I've lost count of the amount of times I've walked right past market stalls wafting the most glorious smells, but when it comes to foreign bacteria I'm a big sissy, so I'm prepared to watch, smell and imagine. Thrill or not, it would be a risk to your system.

For me, thrills and cooking are experiences available to both the cook and the person eating the food. All you need is a little imagination. And some guests with a trusting attitude and the willingness to be experimented upon ...

PEAR SALAD 'N' DILL DRESSING

SERVES 6

175 G/6 OZ MANGE-TOUT PEAS, TOPPED AND TAILED

- STEAM MANGE-TOUT FOR 2 MINUTES TO HEAT.
- DO NOT COOK THROUGH.

DRESSING:

2 TABLESPOONS DILL, CHOPPED

2 TABLESPOONS LEMON JUICE

3 TABLESPOONS DOUBLE CREAM

3 TABLESPOONS VODKA

FRESHLY GROUND BLACK PEPPER

- MIX INGREDIENTS TOGETHER IN A DOWL.
- COVER WARM MANGE-TOUT WITH DRESSING.
- SERVE IMMEDIATELY.

Fiesta Chicken and Salsa
Blessed with Tequila

Serves 6

6 Chicken breasts, skinless

225 ml/8 fl oz/1 cup tequila

Juice of 3 limes

1 tablespoon olive oil

- **Place** chicken and tequila in bowl.
- **Marinate** for 1 hour.
- **Heat** olive oil in pan.
- **Put** chicken in pan to brown and **reserve** tequila.
- **Brown** on both sides.
- **Add** lime juice and tequila.
- **Simmer** over low heat for 20 minutes.
- **Check** chicken is cooked through — flesh must not be pink.
- **Remove** chicken from pan.
- **Turn** heat up high to reduce liquid.
- **Serve** with Salsa Blessed with Tequila.

SALSA:

2 avocados

1 red onion

2 tomatoes, skinned and de-seeded

4 tablespoons olive oil

2 tablespoons cider vinegar

2 tablespoons almonds, chopped

Freshly ground black pepper

2 tablespoons tequila

2 shakes Tabasco sauce

1 bunch fresh coriander

- **Chop** avocado, red onion and tomatoes.
- **Place** in bowl.
- **Add** oil and vinegar.
- **Mix** in almonds and black pepper.
- **Sprinkle** with tequila, Tabasco and chopped coriander.

PEARS POACHED IN RUM

SERVES 6

6 LARGE FIRM PEARS, PEELED

JUICE OF 1 LEMON AND 1 ORANGE

1 STRIP OF ORANGE PEEL

1 STRIP OF LEMON PEEL

1 TABLESPOON DRIED COCONUT

450 ML/16 FL OZ/2 CUPS WHITE RUM

2 TABLESPOONS MAPLE SYRUP

CRÈME FRAÎCHE

- **SLICE** BOTTOMS OFF PEARS AND **STAND UPRIGHT** IN A SAUCEPAN.
- **ADD** JUICE AND **PEEL** OF LEMON AND ORANGE.
- **ADD** COCONUT, RUM AND MAPLE SYRUP.
- **SIMMER** ON LOW HEAT FOR 30 MINUTES OR UNTIL TENDER.
- **TAKE** PEARS OUT AND **ARRANGE** ON WARMED PLATE.
- **REDUCE** LIQUID LEFT IN SAUCEPAN OVER HIGH HEAT TO SYRUPY CONSISTENCY.
- **STRAIN** SAUCE OVER PEARS
- **SERVE** WITH SPOON OF CRÈME FRAÎCHE ON EVERY PEAR.

*To drink: a big Australian Chardonnay; it'd have to be to make an impact!
Good luck!*

UPSET

Women are repeatedly accused of taking things personally. I cannot see any other honest way of taking them.
Marya Mannes

To be deeply upset, or upset at all, can affect us in ways that are quite fundamental. There is not a lot you will actually care about when you are in this state. From global catastrophes to the daily realities of life, all will assume a lesser importance. Even those things so important to daily living will slip and change in their ranking of priority.

One of the ways your body handles this feeling is to put itself into survival mode. You may not even be interested in sitting down to a full meal.

That's fine.

What you will need is the bare essentials to keep life and limb together during this time. That means fluid, vitamins, a certain amount of nutrition and something that is easy to prepare and consume. Don't be worried if your intake is substantially altered during this period, that's perfectly natural.

And as soon as things return to relative normality you can be sure that your normal appetite will return, like a faithful friend.

This is the right time for a Lassi or a Smoothie.

LASSI

SERVES 1

1 BANANA OR 1 PEAR, PEELED

275 ML/10 FL OZ/1 ¼ CUPS MILK OR PLAIN YOGHURT

HONEY TO TASTE

- PUT BANANA OR PEAR IN PROCESSOR.
- ADD MILK OR YOGHURT.
- WHIZZ UNTIL SMOOTH.
- ADD HONEY TO TASTE.
- POUR AND DRINK.

SMOOTHIE

SERVES 2

275 ML/10 FL OZ/1 ¼ CUPS ORANGE JUICE

15 STRAWBERRIES, WASHED AND HULLED

ICE CUBES

- POUR ORANGE JUICE INTO PROCESSOR.
- ADD STRAWBERRIES AND ICE CUBES.
- WHIZZ.
- DRINK.

The combinations are endless: melon and orange, grapefruit and orange, berries and bananas.

To drink: stay off the booze and go for a long walk in the fresh air instead.

VULGAR

I thought Coq au Vin was sex in a car.
Victoria Wood

Remember, vulgarity is in the eye of the beholder. What's vulgar for you might be the height of glamour or screamingly funny for someone else.

Years ago I had the misfortune to be stuck in Shannon Airport on a sweltering summer day, enduring a twelve-hour flight delay to Toronto. We had to disembark and wait in the departure lounge, where there was a bar. I knew trouble was afoot when a large contingent headed straight for the bar and settled in for a marathon drinking session.

I left and went to a nearby hotel for a meal. When I returned to the bar some hours later, a party was in full swing. These travellers were on their annual vacation, and twelve hours in an airport was twelve hours of fun not to be missed out of their holidays. A commendable attitude, you might think, and so did most people, enjoying their high spirits. Some of the airport porters even began to join in the singing.

All of a sudden there was a frenzy of activity as some of the holidaymakers began to go through their suitcases, pulling socks, underwear, jumpers, everything out in their desperate search.

Out came rashers and sausages, black and white pudding and God knows what else. They had decided that the Irish delicacies they had packed to bring on their hols were in danger of levitating. (At that time it was illegal to take the stuff out of the country, so it was being smuggled out wrapped in socks ... Since then, companies devoted to sealing rashers and sausages for unadventurous travellers or homesick emigrés have sprung up.)

Sure enough, in the summer heat of the terminal the contents had begun to go off. The holidaymakers did the obvious thing. They dumped the offending food into rubbish bins around the airport. Some of the more sporting types unwrapped the sausages and began swinging the unravelled lengths around their heads. The air was thick with flying meat products. The Canadians waiting for their flight were thoroughly entertained. But because I travel a lot and the highlight of my trips is to eat the local foods, I found the concept of people packing their own food to take on trips the height of vulgarity.

So what is my idea of vulgar food? White Trash cooking, of course. Invite three of your most vulgar friends around, on condition that they will act and dress in foul taste. The following is adapted from Ernest Matthew Mickler's bible of trashy cuisine, *White Trash Cooking.*

To my mind, cooking methods can be vulgar, and this recipe commits that most vulgar of crimes – adding flour to thicken the sauce.

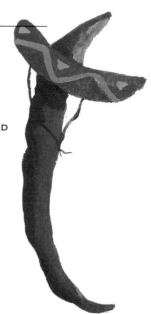

JAILHOUSE CHILLI

SERVES 4

3 TABLESPOONS OLIVE OIL

650 G/1 ½ LB MINCED BEEF

5 TABLESPOONS WATER

4 CHILLI PODS, DE-SEEDED AND CHOPPED
(LESS IF YOU DON'T WANT IT SO FIERY)

3 CLOVES GARLIC, CRUSHED

1 TABLESPOON HONEY

1 TABLESPOON GROUND CUMIN

1 TEASPOON MAJORAM

1 TABLESPOON PAPRIKA

TO THICKEN:

4 TABLESPOONS FLOUR

225 ML/8 FL OZ/1 CUP WATER

- **HEAT** OIL IN LARGE PAN.
- **ADD** MEAT AND **BROWN** OVER HIGH HEAT.
- **ADD** 5 TABLESPOONS WATER AND **COVER**.
- **COOK** OVER VERY LOW HEAT FOR 15 MINUTES.
- **ADD** REMAINING INGREDIENTS, EXCEPT FOR THICKENING.
- **SIMMER** FOR 15 MINUTES.
- **MIX** FLOUR AND WATER, FOR THICKENING, AND **ADD** TO POT.
- **COOK** FOR ANOTHER 5 MINUTES.
- **STIR** TO PREVENT STICKING — MORE WATER MAY BE NEEDED AT THIS POINT IF MIXTURE IS TOO THICK.
- **SERVE** WITH WILD RICE AND **WATCH** THE STEAM ESCAPE FROM YOUR EARS!

And what, I hear you ask, are your vulgar friends and yourself going to be doing while this swamp mixture bubbles? Why, you'll be sipping a coarse cocktail!

SLOW COMFORTABLE SCREW

SERVES 1

1 SHOT GIN

1 SHOT BOURBON

1 GLASS ORANGE JUICE

- **MIX** INGREDIENTS.
- **POUR** OVER ICE.
- **PLACE** A SPARKLER IN DRINK BEFORE SERVING AND **LIGHT**.
- **SIP** WHILE INDULGING IN TRASHY CONVERSATION.

And yes, you are right, this is way too much food for four people. How vulgar!

You can't start worrying about what's going to happen – you get
spastic enough worrying about what's happening now.
Lauren Bacall

Worrying doesn't change anything and it has a negative effect on the body. If you are worrying, stop.

Easier said than done, of course.

Take whatever you are worrying about and run through the worst possible outcome in your head. There, not so bad, is it? If it still is, then throw yourself into some displacement activity. In places like Greece and the Middle East, the men sit around rubbing their worry beads between their fingers, easing their cares away and it seems to work!

So if you're up to high dough, knead that worry away! If nothing else, the smell of baking bread wafting through the house will do your heart good.

BROWN SODA BREAD

MAKES 1 LOAF

450 G/1 LB/4 CUPS WHOLEMEAL FLOUR

1 TEASPOON SEA SALT

2 TABLESPOONS BUTTER

1 TEASPOON BICARBONATE OF SODA

275 ML/10 FL OZ/1 ¼ CUP BUTTERMILK

- PRE-HEAT OVEN TO 200°C/400°F/GAS MARK 6.
- SIFT FLOUR, SALT AND BICARBONATE OF SODA INTO LARGE BOWL.
- RUB IN BUTTER.
- POUR IN BUTTERMILK.
- MIX WITH HANDS INTO DOUGH.
- TURN DOUGH OUT ONTO LIGHTLY FLOURED SURFACE.
- KNEAD INTO A ROUND AND **CUT** A CROSS IN TOP.
- PLACE LOAF ON GREASED TIN.
- BAKE FOR 40-50 MINUTES.
- IF COOKED, BREAD WILL SOUND HOLLOW WHEN TAPPED ON UNDERNEATH.
- PLACE LOAF ON WIRE RACK TO COOL.

WHITE LOAF

MAKES 1 LOAF

750 G/1 ½ LB/6 CUPS STRONG WHITE FLOUR

2 TABLESPOONS BUTTER

1 SACHET (7 G/¼ OZ) EASY-BLEND YEAST OR

FAST ACTION DRIED YEAST

2 TEASPOONS SALT

450 ML/16 FL OZ/2 CUPS WARM WATER

DROP OF OIL

- PRE-HEAT OVEN TO 180°C/370°F/GAS MARK 6.
- SIFT FLOUR INTO BOWL.
- RUB BUTTER IN, USING FINGERTIPS.
- STIR IN YEAST AND SALT.
- POUR IN WARM WATER TO MAKE STIFF DOUGH (YOU MIGHT NOT NEED ALL THE WATER).
- MIX.
- OIL LARGE BOWL.
- KNEAD DOUGH TILL SMOOTH.
- PUT IN BOWL.
- COVER WITH DISHCLOTH.
- LEAVE TO RISE IN WARM PLACE FOR 2 HOURS OR UNTIL DOUGH HAS DOUBLED IN SIZE.
- PLACE DOUGH ON FLOURED SURFACE.
- PUMMEL STRENUOUSLY FOR 4 MINUTES OR UNTIL DOUGH IS ELASTIC AND SMOOTH.
- OIL LARGE BAKING SHEET.
- PLACE DOUGH ON SHEET.
- PLACE IN PLASTIC BAG OR COVER WITH CLINGFILM.
- LEAVE FOR 30 MINUTES IN WARM PLACE UNTIL DOUGH HAS RISEN.
- BAKE FOR 45 MINUTES.
- REMOVE FROM OVEN WHEN GOLDEN BROWN.
- TAP BOTTOM OF LOAF – IF IT SOUNDS HOLLOW, BREAD IS COOKED.
- PLACE LOAF ON WIRE RACK TO COOL.

It does not matter how much or how little we achieve.
If we don't jump for joy about it, we don't feel the emotional mileage.
Astarius Reiki-Om

You've won the lotto. A serious job promotion has come through. Whatever the event, this is a celebratory emotion, one to be shared. Get that cocktail shaker out, there's a cocktail party coming on. And for once, food takes second place.

COCKTAILS

Stick to just two cocktails for reasons of logistics. These two are easy to make, taste delicious and are guaranteed to enhance moments of ecstasy. Strictly for adults only and in moderation.

DELIGHTFUL LIME ZING

SERVES 10

110 ML/4 FL OZ/½ CUP WATER

4 TABLESPOONS MAPLE SYRUP

10 LIMES

1.2 LITRES/2 PINTS/5 CUPS WHITE RUM

CRUSHED ICE

- **POUR** WATER OVER MAPLE SYRUP.
- **JUICE** LIMES.
- **ADD** RUM TO LIMES AND SYRUP.
- **SERVE** OVER CRUSHED ICE WITH SLICE OF LIME.

PINK FLAMINGOES

SERVES 10

1.2 LITRES/2 PINTS/5 CUPS VODKA

JUICE OF 4 PINK GRAPEFRUITS

500 ML/18 FL OZ/2¼ CUPS CRANBERRY JUICE

CRUSHED ICE

- **MIX** EVERYTHING TOGETHER.
- **SERVE** ON CRUSHED ICE.

And anchor that alcohol with the following recipes:

The following quantities should make enough for 10 people:

HUMMUS

225 G/8 OZ/1 ½ CUPS COOKED CHICKPEAS

2 TABLESPOONS TAHINI

3 TABLESPOONS EXTRA VIRGIN OLIVE OIL

3 CLOVES GARLIC, PEELED

3 TABLESPOONS LEMON JUICE

TO EAT WITH THE HUMMUS:

PITTA BREAD

CARROT, CELERY, CUCUMBER CUT IN STRIPS; CAULIFLOWER, IN FLORETS

- **BLEND** CHICKPEAS IN PROCESSOR.
- **ADD** GARLIC, LEMON JUICE, AND **PROCESS** TILL SMOOTH.
- **ADD** TAHINI, AND **WHIZZ** FOR ANOTHER MINUTE.
- **PUT** MIXTURE IN BOWL.
- **SERVE** WITH STRIPS OF PITTA BREAD AND RAW VEGETABLES.

CREAMY AUBERGINE MOUSSE

450 G/1 LB AUBERGINE (EGGPLANT)

6 CLOVES GARLIC

2 EGG YOLKS, FREE RANGE

2 TABLESPOONS LEMON JUICE

FRESHLY GROUND BLACK PEPPER

1 TABLESPOON EXTRA VIRGIN OLIVE OIL

2 TABLESPOONS FRESH CHIVES, CHOPPED

CARROTS AND CELERY IN STRIPS; FLORETS OF CAULIFLOWER

TOASTED PITTA BREAD

- **PRE-HEAT** OVEN TO 180°C/350°F/GAS MARK 4.
- **BAKE** WHOLE, UNPEELED AUBERGINE AND GARLIC CLOVES FOR 45 MINUTES OR UNTIL VERY SOFT.
- **HALVE** AUBERGINE AND **SCOOP OUT** FLESH.
- **PEEL** GARLIC CLOVES.
- **BLEND** AUBERGINE FLESH WITH GARLIC AND EGG YOLKS, LEMON JUICE AND PEPPER.
- **TURN** PROCESSOR TO SLOW AND **ADD** OLIVE OIL.
- **FOLD** IN WHIPPED CREAM.
- **ADD** HALF OF THE CHIVES.
- **SPRINKLE** REST OF CHIVES ON TOP.
- **SERVE** WITH PITTA BREAD FINGERS AND CRUDITÈS IN BASKETS LINED WITH PRETTY COTTON CLOTHS.

BLACK OLIVE PATÉ

450 G/1 LB/2 CUPS BLACK OLIVES

2 TABLESPOONS CAPERS, RINSED

1 CLOVE GARLIC, PEELED

4 TABLESPOONS OLIVE OIL

FRESHLY GROUND BLACK PEPPER

CELERY STICKS

- **PIT** OLIVES.
- **BLEND** ALL INGREDIENTS IN PROCESSOR.
- **SERVE** WITH STICKS OF CELERY.

ANCHOVY BREAD

1 CAN (50 G/2 OZ) ANCHOVY FILLETS

3 TABLESPOONS OLIVE OIL

2 CLOVES GARLIC, PEELED

FRESHLY GROUND BLACK PEPPER

LARGE LOAF OF UNSLICED BREAD

- **DRAIN** ANCHOVY FILLETS.
- **SOAK** IN WATER FOR 1 HOUR TO REDUCE SALT CONTENT.
- **DRAIN** ON KITCHEN PAPER.
- **BLEND** ALL INGREDIENTS TOGETHER.
- **SLICE** LOAF IN HALF LENGTHWAYS.
- **SPREAD** ANCHOVY PASTE ON HALVES.
- **PLACE** UNDER GRILL.
- **GRILL** UNTIL ANCHOVY PASTE BUBBLES.
- **REMOVE.**
- **SANDWICH** HALVES TOGETHER AND **SLICE**.
- **SERVE** WHILE HOT.

As long as you can still be disappointed you are still young.
Sarah Churchill

You're as young as you feel, or so the saying goes. There is a grain of truth to this, but there are also several foods out there that can help you feel – and look – younger.

Drinking plenty of water to wash out toxins and keep the complexion clear is crucial to feeling and looking youthful.

Fresh fruit and vegetables are also vital.

And to help the skin-deep part of beauty, how about applying food externally?

It's great to make up your own face mask. You know exactly what's going in and for people like me with very sensitive skin that's a real bonus. *And* a home-made facial treatment is a real money-saver. Try this one on – it's a great exfoliant and is suitable for all skin types. Cut slices of cool cucumber, place them over your eyes and lie back and relax.

FEED YOUR FACE MASK

2 TABLESPOONS COARSE MARMALADE

2 TABLESPOONS GROUND ALMONDS

- MIX THESE INGREDIENTS TOGETHER.
- SPREAD ON FACE.
- LEAVE FOR 10 MINUTES.
- MASSAGE WITH TIPS OF FINGERS USING CIRCULAR MOTIONS.
- WASH OFF WITH LUKEWARM WATER.

Another great exfoliant mask: AHAs (alpha-hydroxy acids) are the cosmetic companies' great new discovery. There are high levels of AHA lactic acid in yoghurt, and malic acid in apples which help stimulate the skin and regenerate the cells to help keep you youthful.

YOGHURT AND APPLE MASK

FOR ALL SKIN TYPES

2 TABLESPOONS YOGHURT

1 APPLE, SHREDDED

- **MIX** YOGHURT AND APPLE TOGETHER.
- **SPREAD** ON FACE.
- **LEAVE** FOR 10 MINUTES.
- **WASH OFF** WITH LUKEWARM WATER.

Avocado is full of oil and makes a very soothing facial:

AVOCADO AND HONEY MASK

FOR ALL SKIN TYPES

1 RIPE AVOCADO

1 TABLESPOON HONEY

- **MASH** AVOCADO.
- **MIX** WITH HONEY.
- **SPREAD** ON FACE.
- **LEAVE** FOR 10 MINUTES.
- **WASH OFF** WITH LUKEWARM WATER.

EGGY HAIR SOUP

1 EGG

1 TABLESPOON OLIVE OIL

- **WHIZZ** IN PROCESSOR.
- **WASH** HAIR AND **RINSE** IN WARM WATER.
- **RUB** MIXTURE INTO SCALP.
- **COVER** WITH WARM TOWEL AND **LEAVE** FOR 20 MINUTES.
- **MASSAGE** BEFORE RINSING OFF.
- **USE** EXCEEDINGLY GENTLE SHAMPOO, WHICH IS ACID BALANCED, TO RINSE OFF.
- **LET** HAIR **DRY** NATURALLY.

ZESTFUL

Life without zest is like champagne without bubbles.
Anon

This is a mood that makes you want to splash through the puddle as you walk along. Without knowing who has called you on the phone, you'll answer with a cheery greeting and continue in that vein, even if it is the credit card company threatening to pull the plug.

Nothing can or will get you down, and in fact you can even positively affect the outcome of certain situations that would normally get on your nerves.

It's infectious, and people love it.

The bottom line is that it's a zest for life. It's not difficult to identify zestful food, the whole citrus family are definites – there's a tang in those fruits that will tingle your taste buds.

Chilled Pepper 'n' Lime Soup

Serves 4

10 RED PEPPERS

1 CAN PLUM TOMATOES

570 ML/1 PINT/2 ½ CUPS VEGETABLE STOCK

FRESHLY GROUND BLACK PEPPER

TABASCO TO TASTE

JUICE OF 4 LIMES

ZEST OF 2 LIMES

BUNCH OF FRESH MINT

- **ROAST** RED PEPPERS ON BAKING TRAY IN OVEN AT 180°C/350°F/GAS MARK 4 FOR 30 MINUTES OR UNTIL SKIN ON PEPPERS IS BLISTERED AND BROWN.

- **TAKE** PEPPERS OUT.

- **PUT** INTO POLYTHENE BAG.

- **SEAL** FOR 30 MINUTES.

- **TAKE OUT** AND **PEEL** SKIN OFF.

- **PLACE** FLESH OF PEPPERS, PLUM TOMATOES AND VEGETABLE STOCK IN PROCESSOR.

- **ADD** PEPPER AND TABASCO TO TASTE.

- **POUR** INTO BOWL.

- **PLACE** IN FRIDGE TO CHILL FOR ABOUT 2 HOURS.

- **BEFORE** SERVING, **STIR** IN LIME JUICE.

- **PLACE** SLICE OF LIME ON EDGE OF SOUP BOWL.

- **SPRINKLE** ZEST OF LIMES ON TOP.

- **GARNISH** WITH SPRIG OF MINT ON TOP.

Citrus Sole

Serves 4

ZEST AND JUICE OF 1 LIME

ZEST AND JUICE OF 1 LEMON

4 MEDIUM-SIZED LEMON SOLE

4 TABLESPOONS OLIVE OIL

- **PRE-HEAT** OVEN TO 180°C/350°F/GAS MARK 4.

- **PLACE** EACH SOLE IN A LARGE PIECE OF TIN FOIL.

- **BEFORE** SEALING **POUR** 1 TABLESPOON OF OLIVE OIL, AND A LITTLE LIME AND LEMON JUICE ON EACH FISH.

- **SEASON** WITH PEPPER.

- **SEAL** PARCELS BY TWISTING TINFOIL.

- **PLACE** IN OVEN FOR 20 MINUTES.

- **HEAT** REMAINING CITRUS JUICES AND ZEST IN SAUCEPAN.

- **SIMMER** OVER HIGH HEAT TO REDUCE LIQUID BY HALF.

- **REMOVE** SOLE FROM TINFOIL, PUT ON PLATES AND POUR SAUCE OVER FISH.

- **SERVE** WITH LEMON-SCENTED RICE.

LEMON-SCENTED RICE

SERVES 4
225 G/8 OZ/1 $\frac{1}{4}$ CUPS WHITE RICE

570 ML/1 PINT/2 $\frac{1}{2}$ CUPS BOILING WATER

3 BAY LEAVES

5 GREEN CARDAMOM PODS

3 THREADS SAFFRON OR $\frac{1}{2}$ TEASPOON POWDERED SAFFRON

JUICE OF 3 LEMONS

- **RINSE** RICE IN COLD WATER.

- **PLACE** IN LARGE PAN WITH BOILING WATER.

- **ADD** BAY LEAVES, CARDAMOM PODS AND SAFFRON.

- **COVER** WITH LID AND **SIMMER** FOR 15 MINUTES.

- **RICE** SHOULD BE COOKED WHEN LIQUID HAS BEEN ABSORBED.

- **REMOVE** BAY LEAVES AND CARDAMOM PODS.

- **PLACE** RICE IN WARMED SERVING DISH.

- **STIR** IN LEMON JUICE.

- **BEFORE** SERVING, **FLUFF** RICE UP WITH FORK.

Zesty Crêpes

CRÊPES:

115 g/4 oz/⅔ cup flour

1 free range egg

110 ml/4 fl oz/½ cup milk

⅛ teaspoon grated nutmeg

½ teaspoon vanilla extract

Zest of 1 orange

Sunflower oil

- **Put** flour into bowl.
- **Add** egg.
- **Start** whisking.
- **Mix** in milk gradually.
- **Continue whisking** until you have a batter.
- **Add** in nutmeg, vanilla and orange zest.
- **Cover** batter and **put aside** for 30 minutes.
- **Heat** an 20 cm/8 inch non-stick pan.
- **Put** drop of olive oil on pan.
- **Spoon** enough batter to form a thin layer onto pan.
- **Cook** for 2 minutes and then **flip over** to other side.
- **Continue to cook** for a further 2 minutes.
- **Remove** crêpe and **place** on plate in warm oven.
- **Place** a sheet of grease-proof paper between each crêpe.
- **Continue** process for other 7 crêpes.

SAUCE:

570 ml/1 pint/2½ cups orange juice

2 tablespoons Cointreau

1 teaspoon honey

1 tablespoon orange zest

1 tablespoon lime zest

Dollop of crème fraîche

- **COMBINE** ORANGE JUICE, HALF OF ZEST AND HONEY IN NON-STICK PAN.
- **REDUCE** LIQUID TO SYRUPY CONSISTENCY ON HIGH HEAT.
- **LAY** CRÊPES ON INDIVIDUAL SERVING DISHES.
- **STIR** COINTREAU INTO SAUCE.
- **POUR** SAUCE OVER CRÊPES.
- **SERVE** WITH SPOONFUL OF CRÈME FRAÎCHE MIXED WITH REMAINING GRATED RIND.
- **HEY ZESTO!**

To drink: Make a jug of margharitas to sip throughout the meal

MARGHARITA SPRINGS

SERVES 4

225 ML/8 FL OZ/1 CUP TEQUILA

55 ML/2 FL OZ/$\frac{1}{4}$ CUP COINTREAU

225 ML/8 FL OZ/1 CUP LIME JUICE

CRUSHED ICE

LIME SLICES TO SERVE

- **PUT** TEQUILA, COINTREAU, LIME JUICE AND ICE IN PROCESSOR.
- **WHIZZ** UNTIL SMOOTH.
- **SERVE** WITH SLICE OF LIME ON SIDE.
- **SIP** AND **ZING** YOUR WAY TO ZESTFULNESS.

INDEX

A

ALL STEAMED-UP SEAFOOD 104

ALMOND AND ORANGE PIE 77

ANCHOVY
bread 127
dressing 23

APPLES, BAKED 85

APRICOT JUICE see SUNSTROKE 109

ASPARAGUS SOUP 71

AUBERGINE
mousse 125
spiced 25

AVOCADO
and Honey Mask 129
soup 36

B

BACK TO ROOTS VEG 92

BAKED APPLES 85

BANANA
bread 78
flambéed 19
shake 116

BEEF, SIZZLING STIR-FRY 16

BELLINI COCKTAIL 45

BLACK OLIVE PATÉ 126

BLAST FROM THE PAST 109

BLISSFUL BLOODY MARYS 21

BLUE SKIES PEPPERS 95

BOURBON see SLOW COMFORTABLE SCREW 120

BRANDY see SUNSTROKE 109

BREAD AND BUTTER PUD 93

BREADS AND CAKES
Almond and Orange Pie 77
Anchovy Bread 127
Banana Bread 78
Brown Soda Bread 121
Scones 80
Teacakes 79
White Loaf 122

BROWN LENTIL SOUP 60

BROWN SODA BREAD 121

BRUSSEL SPROUTS, STIR-FRIED 84

BURGERS, LAMB 57

C

CABBAGE WITH POTATOES 92

CALMING COUSCOUS 29

CARROT
soup 107
with couscous 29

CELEBRATION LAMB 47

CELERY
Courgette and Parsley Salad 33
Juice 111

CHAMPAGNE
with peaches 46
risotto 40

CHEERFUL CARROT SOUP 107

CHEESE DISHES
al fresco 96
cheeses 27
chicken breasts stuffed with goat's cheese 69
cucumber sandwiches 76
feta and leeks wrapped in filo pastry 46
figs cooked with honey and brandy 24
risotto with chicken 61
Sophisticates' Soufflé 32

CHICKEN DISHES
Fiesta and Salsa Blessed with Tequila 114
lemon-roasted 84
Moroccan 28
paella with mussels, clams and prawns 52

risotto with parmesan 61
steamed chicken breasts stuffed with goat's
    cheese 69
tortillas 21

CHICKPEAS 125
CHILLED PEPPER 'N' LIME SOUP
    132
CHILLI 119
CHOCOLATE
mousse, Guilt-Free Chocolate Cream 49
pudding, OTT Pudding 43
strawberries smothered in chocolate 13

CITRUS SOLE 132
CLAMS
paella with chicken, mussels and prawns 52
steamed with prawns and
    mussels 104

COCKTAILS
Blast from the Past 109
Blissful Bloody Marys 21
Delightful Lime Zing 124
Margharita Springs 135
Orange Vodka 106
Pink Flamingoes 124
Slow Comfortable Screw 120
Sunburst 109
Sunstroke 109
Welcome Drink 46

COINTREAU see MARGHARITA
    SPRINGS 135
COLCANNON 92
COMPOTE, HOT FRUIT 66
CORN CHOWDER 56
COURGETTE AND PARSLEY SALAD
    33
COUSCOUS AND CARROTS 29
CRANBERRY JUICE see PINK
    FLAMINGOES 124
CREAMY AUBERGINE MOUSSE 125
CREAMY DREAMY PORRIDGE 35
CREAMY PEA SOUP 64
CREAMY VEGETABLE SOUP 83

CRÊPES WITH ORANGE AND COIN
    TREAU SAUCE 134
CUCUMBER
Salad with mango 13
with cream cheese 76

CUNNING CORN CHOWDER 56
CURRIED VEGETABLES 17

D
DELIGHTFUL LIME ZING 124
DILL DRESSING 113

E
EGG DISHES
Eggy Hair Soup 129
omelette with potatoes and
    onions 95
Oriental Quail's Eggs 87
Sophisticates' Soufflé 32
Spanish omelette 15
with Attitude 15
with salmon on muffin 99

EMERALD SALAD 37

F
FACE MASKS
avocado and honey 129
marmalade and almond 128
yoghurt and apple 129
Feed your Face Mask 128

FETA CHEESE AND LEEKS
    WRAPPED IN FILO
    PASTRY 46

FIESTA CHICKEN AND SALSA
    BLESSED WITH
    TEQUILA 114

FIGS WITH HONEY, BRANDY AND
    CHEESE 24

FILO PASTRY WITH LEEKS
    AND CHEESE 46

FISH DISHES
lobster with lime butter 42

Mussel Mania 22
Passionfruit Prawns 12
Poached Wild Salmon with Mint
    Hollandaise Sauce 72
salmon and eggs on muffin 99
Smoked Mackerel Paté 76
smoked salmon with tagliatelle 65
sole baked with citrus 132
steamed prawns 96
steamed shellfish with soy sauce 104
white fish grilled 100

FLAMING BANANAS 19
FROTHY FRUIT JUICE 97
FRUIT
    apples, baked 85
    compote 66
    figs with honey, brandy and cheese 24
    kebabs with cashew nut cream 101
    nectarines 53
    passionfruit with yoghurt 99
    pears in rum 115
    prunes cooked in port 48
    raspberry fool 70
    salad with melon, kiwi and grapes 37
    salad, mixed 112

G

GALLIANO see BLAST FROM THE
    PAST 109
GAZPACHO 51
GIN see SLOW COMFORTABLE
    SCREW 120
GRAPEFRUIT
    and orange juice 97
    Pink Flamingoes 124
GRAPES WITH MELON AND KIWI 37
GREEN-EYED SOUP 36
GRILLED FISH AND VEGETABLES
    100
GUILT-FREE CHOCOLATE CREAM 49

H

HAIR MASK 129

HAZELNUT
    dressing 96
    ice cream 73

HEAVENLY FIGS 24
HONEY MOUSSE 58
HOT FRUIT COMPOTE 66
HUMMUS 125

I

ICE CREAM WITH HAZELNUTS 73
IRISH STEW 91

J

JAILHOUSE CHILLI 119
JUICE, CELERY 111
JUICE, FROTHY FRUIT 97

K

KIWI WITH MELON AND GRAPES 37
KITCHEN SINK TOMATO SANDWICH
    88

L

LAMB
    and rice-stuffed peppers 108
    burgers 57
    Irish stew 91
    roast with rosemary 47

LASSI 116

LEEKS AND FETA CHEESE
    WRAPPED IN FILO PASTRY 46
LEMON ROASTED CHICKEN 84
LEMON-SCENTED RICE 133
LENTIL SOUP 60
LETTUCE-WRAPPED CHICKEN
    BREASTS STUFFED WITH GOAT'S
    CHEESE 69
LIFE-SAVING SOUP 34
LIME
    chilled pepper soup 132

Delightful Lime Zing 124
lobster with lime butter 42
Margharita Springs 135
Lobster 'n' Lime 42

LOBSTER, RULES FOR COOKING 41

M

MANGO
salad with cucumber 13
sorbet 108
sunburst 109

MARGHARITA SPRINGS 135
MASCARPONE CHEESE WITH FIGS 24
MELON WITH KIWI AND GRAPES 37
MINT
hollandaise sauce 72
tea 30

MISO
choosing 34
soup 34

MOROCCAN CHICKEN 28
MUM'S BAKED APPLES 85
MUSHROOM
Cappuccino 68
Sauce, Wild 57

MUSSELS
paella with chicken, clams and prawns 52
sautéed in white wine 22
steamed with prawns and clams 104

N

NECTARINA NIRVANA 53
NOODLES WITH POPPY SEEDS 62
NUTTY ICE CREAM 73

O

OIRISH STEW 91
OLIVE PATÉ 126
OMELETTE
Spanish 15
with potatoes and onions 95

ORANGES
and cointreau sauce 134
and grapefruit juice 97
crêpes 134
juice in a screw 120
juice with brandy 109
pancakes 98
pie with almond crust 77
shake with strawberries 117
vodka 106

ORIENTAL QUAIL'S EGGS 87
OTT PUDDING 43
OUTDOORS OMELETTE 95
OYSTER SOUP 11

P

PAELLA WITH CHICKEN, MUSSELS, CLAMS AND PRAWNS 52
PANCAKES 98
PARADISICAL PAELLA 52
PARMESAN
in risotto 61
in soufflé 32

PARSNIP PIE SURPRISE 89
PASSIONFRUIT
with prawns 12
with yoghurt 99

PASTA DISHES
pesto 37
smoked salmon 65

PATÉS
black olive 126
smoked mackerel 76

PEA SOUP 64
PEACH
juice with tequila, galliano and vodka 109
with champagne 46

PEARS POACHED IN RUM 115

PEPPERS
chilled lime soup 132
salad, mixed 95
salad, roasted 23
soufflé 32
stuffed with rice and lamb 108

PESTO PASTA 37
PICNIC PRAWNS 96
PIES
almond crust and orange cream 77
parsnip 89

PINK FLAMINGOES 124
POACHED WILD SALMON WITH
MINT HOLLANDAISE SAUCE 72
POPPY SEED
dressing 27
with noodles 62

PORTLY PRUNES 48
PORRIDGE 35
POTATOES
asparagus soup 71
Irish stew 91
omelette with potatoes and
onions 95
omelette, Spanish 15
with anchovies, Dijon mustard and gherkins
23
with cabbage 92

PRAWNS
paella with chicken, mussels and clams 52
steamed with clams and mussels 104
with passionfruit 12

PRUNES COOKED IN PORT 48
PUDDINGS
bread and butter 93
OTT, with chocolate and coffee 43
steamed raisin 105

Q
QUAIL
eggs 87
with wild mushrooms 26

R
RAISIN PUDDING 105
RASPBERRY SOUP 70
RED PEPPERS AS SOUFFLÉ DISH
32
RICE DISHES
Champagne Risotto 40
Chicken Risotto 61
Lemon-Scented Rice 133
Paradisical Paella 52
Sunny Peppers 108

RIOT RAISIN' PUDDING 105
ROARING RED SALSA 16
ROAST VEGETABLES 48
ROASTED PEPPER SALAD 23
RUM
Delightful Lime Zing 124
poached pears 115

S
SALADS
Blue Skies Peppers 95
courgette and parsley 33
mango and cucumber 13
roasted pepper 23
salsa blessed with tequila 114
simple 112
warm with dill dressing 113
with poppy seed dressing 27

SALSA BLESSED WITH TEQUILA
114
SANDWICHES
cucumber and cream cheese 76
tomato 88

SAUCES & DRESSINGS
Anchovy Dressing 23
Dill Dressing 113

Hazelnut Dressing 96
Mint Hollandaise Sauce 72
Orange and cointreau sauce 134
Poppy Seed Dressing 27
Roaring Red Salsa 16
Vinaigrette 112
Wild Mushroom Sauce 57

SCONES 80
SIMPLE SALAD 112
SIZZLING STIR-FRY BEEF 16
SLOW COMFORTABLE SCREW 120
SMOKED MACKEREL PATÉ 76
SMOKED SALMON PASTA 65
SMOOTHIE 117
SOPHISTICATES' SOUFFLÉ 32
SORBET 108
SOUFFLÉ
rules for making 31
Soufflé, Sophisticates' 32

SOUPS
Asparagus Soup 71
Brown Lentil Soup 60
Cheerful Carrot Soup 107
Chilled Pepper 'n' Lime Soup 132
Creamy Pea Soup 64
Creamy Vegetable Soup 83
Cunning Corn Chowder 56
Gazpacho 51
Green-Eyed Soup 36
Life-Saving Soup 34
Mushroom Cappuccino 68
Oyster Soup 11

SPICED AUBERGINE 25
STICKY HONEY CREAM 58
STIR-FRYS
sizzling beef 16
Brussels sprouts 84

STRAWBERRIES
and orange shake 117
chocolate-smothered 13

STUFFED PEPPERS 108

SUCCULENT SALMON 99
SUNBURST 109
SUNNY PEPPERS 108
SUNSTROKE 109
SURPRISE PARCELS 46

T
TAGLIATELLE WITH SMOKED
SALMON 65
TEA
choosing 74
mint 30

TEACAKES 79
TEQUILA
Blast from the Past 109
Margharita Springs 135

TOMATOES
Bloody Marys 21
gazpacho 51
sandwich 88
TORTILLAS STUFFED WITH
CHICKEN, SALSA AND SOUR
CREAM 21
TRICKY QUAIL 26
TRIPLE SEC see SUNBURST 109
TURNIPS WITH ONIONS 92
TUTTI-FRUITTI 112

V
VEGETABLE DISHES
Back to Roots Veg 92
Colcannon 92
Creamy Aubergine Mousse 125
Cucumber Sandwiches 76
curried 17
grilled 100
Kitchen Sink Tomato Sandwich 88
Potatoes with Anchovy Dressing 23
roasted 48
Sophisticates' Soufflé 32
Spiced Aubergine 25
Stir-Fry Brussels Sprouts 84

Vegetable Soup 83
Vinaigrette 112
VODKA
Blast from the Past 109
Blissful Bloody Marys 21
Pink Flamingoes 124
with orange juice 106

W
WARM SALAD 'N' DILL DRESSING
113
WELCOME DRINK 46

WHISKEY *see* SUNBURST 109
WHITE LOAF 122
WILD MUSHROOM SAUCE 57

Y
YOGHURT AND APPLE MASK 129
YOGHURT, WITH PASSIONFRUIT 99

Z
ZESTY CRÊPES 134